Withdrawn

3 9082 12199 6337

W9-BVA-194

Praise for Garret Kramer's
STILLPOWER

"As I reflect back on my personal quest to develop character through the sport of football, I greatly identify with the wisdom and principles of this book. *Stillpower* is a profound playbook for the athletic and life journey. Garret Kramer shows us that people become what they think in their heart, not in their head."

TYRONE KEYS, FOUNDER OF ALL SPORTS COMMUNITY SERVICES, SUPER BOWL–WINNING DEFENSIVE END—CHICAGO BEARS

. . .

"Garret Kramer understands the importance of having your head right. *Stillpower* reveals the optimum mental functioning of an athlete and the real source of that functioning. Under this paradigm, individuals involved in sports will enjoy the character-building benefits often promised by participation. Even children will find athletics more enjoyable and, at the same time, achieve high levels of success. I know this may all sound like a tall order, but this book honestly offers that potential."

GEORGE PRANSKY, PHD

"I was first introduced to sports psychology in the 1970s when I was playing professional baseball. Like all athletes, I was constantly in search of that magical place called 'the zone,' where the game slows down and pitches are suddenly easy to track. Contrary to what most people think, however, finding your way to 'the zone' doesn't come from grinding or strength of will—it comes from another source. *Stillpower* reveals this surprising source. If you're a serious athlete, coach, sports parent—in fact, anyone—I strongly suggest you read what Garret Kramer has to say about getting to the top of your game, on and off the field."

RICK WOLFF, SPORTS PSYCHOLOGY EXPERT AND HOST OF *THE SPORTS EDGE*, WFAN RADIO, NEW YORK

• • •

"I first heard Garret Kramer speak in 2009, and I was instantly intrigued by his message and approach to athletic mental performance. *Stillpower* takes a unique perspective that will challenge your traditional beliefs. If you keep an open mind and really listen to what this book has to say, you will realize how much easier and more positive life can be, and why the notion of 'no pain, no gain' will never help in your pursuit of success."

ROB NADDELMAN, PRESIDENT OF BASEBALL FACTORY

"The message introduced in this book is the reverse of any mental strategy or technique that I have ever tried. *Stillpower* has shown me that my thoughts and moods create my perceptions. So, instead of being victimized by my circumstances, I determine my own performance level—no matter what is happening outside of me. As a result of understanding the principles of thought and consciousness, I now find myself in 'the zone' way more often. Thanks to Garret Kramer I just had the best year of my professional career."

COLIN WILSON, NASHVILLE PREDATORS FORWARD

. . .

"I have often invited Garret Kramer to speak to our elite prep athletes throughout the country. He has opened their minds to a new way of looking at performance. He has taught them that free will is the number one ingredient for success on and off the football field. Take your time reading *Stillpower*. These thoughtful lessons will change the way you look at the athletic journey. This book is invaluable to anyone who wants to perform better in the heat of competition."

RICHARD MCGUINNESS, PRESIDENT OF FOOTBALL UNIVERSITY, CREATOR AND PRODUCER OF THE US ARMY ALL-AMERICAN BOWL ON NBC

"Garret Kramer has refused to accept preexisting concepts about understanding the cerebral part of athletic competition. Through perceptive analysis and examples, *Stillpower* unlocks a thought-provoking and groundbreaking approach. Over the past three decades, I have been fortunate to observe, from close range, thousands of athletes and coaches in their pursuit of excellence. All of them could benefit from reading this book, not only to reach new heights on the playing field but in their lives away from the game as well."

ROB COWEN, NINE-TIME EMMY AWARD–WINNING
SPORTS TELEVISION PRODUCER

. . .

"Having represented professional athletes for more than twenty-five years, it isn't often you come across a book so crucial for an athlete. From high school and college prospects to the pros, *Stillpower* provides athletes a unique edge. In a counterintuitive sense, Garret Kramer takes the player back to a childlike and free state of mind, where external circumstances are irrelevant. The inner peace and mind-set that an athlete can achieve through the understanding revealed in this book can transform the athlete and create a happier day-to-day existence, eventually allowing the player to become extremely effective in the game."

JAY GROSSMAN, PRESIDENT OF PUCKAGENCY, LLC

STILLPOWER

STILLPOWER

EXCELLENCE WITH EASE
IN SPORTS AND LIFE

GARRET KRAMER

ATRIA BOOKS
New York London Toronto Sydney New Delhi

BEYOND WORDS
Hillsboro, Oregon

ATRIA BOOKS
A Division of Simon & Schuster, Inc.
1230 Avenue of the Americas
New York, NY 10020

BEYOND WORDS
20827 N.W. Cornell Road, Suite 500
Hillsboro, Oregon 97124-9808
503-531-8700 / 503-531-8773 fax
www.beyondword.com

Copyright © 2011 by Garret Kramer

Originally published in 2011 by Greenleaf Book Group Press,
ISBN 978-1-60832-185-8

All rights reserved, including the right to reproduce this book or portions thereof in any form whatsoever without the prior written permission of Atria Books/Beyond Words Publishing, Inc., except where permitted by law.

Design: Rodrigo Corral Design and Devon Smith (Beyond Words)
Composition: William H. Brunson Typography Services

First Atria Books/Beyond Words hardcover edition June 2012

ATRIA BOOKS and colophon are trademarks of Simon & Schuster, Inc. Beyond Words Publishing is an imprint of Simon & Schuster, Inc., and the Beyond Words logo is a registered trademark of Beyond Words Publishing, Inc.

For more information about special discounts for bulk purchases, please contact Simon & Schuster Special Sales at 1-866-506-1949 or business@simonandschuster.com.

The Simon & Schuster Speakers Bureau can bring authors to your live event. For more information or to book an event, contact the Simon & Schuster Speakers Bureau at 1-866-248-3049 or visit our website at www.simonspeakers.com.

Manufactured in the United States of America

10 9 8 7 6 5 4 3 2 1

Library of Congress Cataloging-in-Publication Data

Kramer, Garret.
    Stillpower : excellence with ease in sports and life / Garret Kramer.
        p. cm.
    Includes bibliographical references and index.
        1. Sports—Psychological aspects. 2. Athletes—Psychology.
    3. Competition (Psychology). I. Title.
    GV706.4.K72   2011
    796.01—dc23
                                                                2012001696

ISBN 978-1-58270-388-6
ISBN 978-1-4516-8869-6 (ebook)

The corporate mission of Beyond Words Publishing, Inc.: *Inspire to Integrity*

To Ellie—Words cannot adequately describe my love for you. Thank you for understanding the principles behind contentment and success. You've shown me the way.

CONTENTS

FOREWORD

BY ZACH PARISE

NHL ALL-STAR AND MEMBER OF THE US OLYMPIC HOCKEY TEAM

I feel privileged to write the foreword for this book. When I first met Garret Kramer in September 2008, I realized that I was being introduced to an entirely new, yet simple, approach to my performance as a professional athlete. More important, I immediately saw the connection between the thoughts in my head and how I was feeling in my life away from the game. Then, as I became more aware of the principles that Garret teaches, I began to notice a greater sense of calm in everything I did. This peacefulness didn't hit me right away, but day by day, as I learned more, it seemed to grow. Garret insists that this "understanding," as he often calls it, has been inside me all along. While that may or may not be true, I know that my highs now happen more often, and when the lows do occur, they don't seem to last so long.

Throughout my life as a hockey player, I have been introduced to a lot of mental approaches—different tools, techniques, and exercises. To be honest, none of them worked with any regularity. For example, I often wondered why visualizing success on the ice would work one day but not another. Why before one game I could quiet my nerves, but the next night my thoughts wouldn't settle. I now understand why this is the case. Garret helped me to see that my performance is dependent on my own thoughts and feelings, not on anything that is happening outside of me. So, come game time (or during any situation), I now realize I am capable of playing well or feeling good, no matter what is going on at home, in the dressing room, or in the arena. It is no accident that I have had the best two years of my career since I started working with Garret, and I feel fortunate to call him a friend.

One word of advice as you read this book: Do not attempt to memorize the information. During my first meeting with Garret, I arrived with a notepad and pen. A friend who worked with Garret had told me about all the cool stuff we were going to talk about so I didn't want to miss a thing. Well, right off, Garret told me to put the pen down. He said I should draw my own conclusions and listen to the feeling of what he was saying, and to not think so much. That is what you should do as you read along here. You will see that Garret is consistent in what he says. He uses many examples and makes connections between them to reinforce the message in different ways. You won't even realize it, but before you know it, you will be applying his lessons to your own athletic career or to life in general. You will understand how your mind works and how successful and happy people steer easily through their lives.

I believe the principles introduced in this book are the future of athletic mental performance—actually, performance of any kind. Garret helped me to recognize that in grinding so hard, I was reducing my chances to perform up to my capabilities. Now I see why the game wasn't always as enjoyable as I wanted it to be. Today, my effort is present like before, but for some reason it rarely feels like work, and I am simply more successful in everything that I do.

In *Stillpower*, Garret offers hope for discovering our potential to perform freely, regardless of the circumstances of our lives. I hope, like me, you find this perspective to be extremely valuable.

PREFACE

I am about to make an odd proposal, especially for a coach: As you begin reading this book, *do not* try hard to grasp the concepts. I know, you are convinced that trying hard, or extraordinary effort, is essential for success. Well, hold that thought for now, go with my suggestion, and let's see where the dust ultimately settles.

To be clear, it's not that I don't want you to learn as you read my words; it's that I don't want you to *study* them. Like the best athletes in their finest moments, I hope you will turn off your intellect and just absorb the ideas in this book. Don't worry; it won't be a long or terribly complex process. As an athlete, coach, sports parent—or anyone looking to improve his or her life— you will soon be introduced to a revolutionarily *simple* paradigm for performance. So simple that if you happen to get stuck as you move along, if you start to overthink or grind, my advice is to put the book down—back-burner the concept, if you will—and come back to it later. Again, if you try too hard, I fear that the feeling behind what I'm saying might get lost. For success in any endeavor (especially athletics), it's all about the feeling anyway. And we can never find the right feeling when we try to force it.

There is one other suggestion that I want to make early on: If, in spite of being absorbed and feeling present, you still think you might not be grasping the recurrent theme of *Stillpower*, just hang in there. You already have *within you* all that is necessary for enduring success. As philosopher and author Sydney Banks, one of my mentors, once said, "Happiness is only *one thought away*—but first you must find, for yourself, that one thought."[1] It may become visible as you read the introduction, the last chapter, or even as you're driving down the road a month from now. So, turn away from the temptation to judge any initial uncertainty. I am sure that at the appropriate time for you—the answers will appear.

Like many individuals, I once believed that employing willpower was an integral part of the human experience. I was proud to say it defined me as an athlete, coach, parent, and member of society. Today, I look back and wonder, *What was I actually thinking? Why was I making the athletic experience so much more difficult, both mentally and physically, than it needed to be? Why was I inhibiting my own success?* Shortly, you will find out the answers for yourself. As for me, every day I learn more and go deeper. Now I feel extremely fortunate to share this quest with you.

Thank you for opening your heart to this fresh yet fundamental perspective. My hope is that you reflect on these words and find their message as insightful and productive as I do.

INTRODUCTION

Stillpower: *The clarity of mind to live with freedom and ease; the inner source of excellence; the opposite of willpower.*
GARRET KRAMER

For the past ten years, athletes, coaches, and parents have listened to my talks, read my articles, or traveled to my coaching and consulting company—Inner Sports—to discover the psychological strategies necessary to improve individual or team performance. Usually these individuals want to feel better and play more proficiently. Often they seek the answers to success, but always they are surprised by what I teach.

Why are they surprised? Because my initial message is that external strategies, like all how-to techniques, are ineffective. If a person is struggling and attempts to force a fix, his or her confidence, energy, and attitude will only get worse.

Yet, far removed from this standard approach, what you can learn at Inner Sports, and from this book, too, is how every person shapes his or her experience: One's state of mind will determine his or her outlook. Then, once learned, this understanding will lead you straight to your inner source of excellence—something I call *stillpower*.

Stillpower is pain free, yet so dynamic it has the potential to change your life—both on and off the playing field. It revolves around a deep faith in your inner wisdom and innate resilience; in trusting that all sentiments are temporary since they originate from your own thoughts and moods. Stillpower comes from knowing that self-worth has nothing to do with winning, losing, parent approval, money, fame, or anything external to you.

To put it simply, I believe that the finest competitors in every sport play with stillpower—not willpower. To them, trying hard and giving their best effort are not the same thing. These athletes feel a sense of cooperation with—and respect for—their teammates, coaches, and even opponents, thus mental clarity is their norm. Men and women with stillpower excel in many fields and develop into our most prolific leaders. They naturally gravitate to their passions, rarely feel fatigued, and intuitively know what *not to do* if they happen to drift off course.

While stillpower's promise might be hard for you to appreciate at this stage of the game, for me it rings true. One day I looked in this freeing direction and never looked back again.

. . .

Like many coaches, I grew up in a world where being an athlete was as natural as breathing. I was an all-state ice hockey player in high school and had a successful college career. In my early twenties, I took up the game of golf and was fortunate enough to qualify for four USGA championships. To be honest, I was never the fastest or most talented player on the ice or in the tournament. But I loved the competition that these sports provided, especially the journey surrounding the contests. It was during the process of training, practicing, and interacting with teammates where I uncovered a state of mind that allowed me to find success, no matter what circumstances I faced. This concept is at the heart of this book.

I also learned early in my life that I enjoyed coaching, whether as a counselor at Camp Kenwood in Wilmot,

New Hampshire, or running hockey clinics at Ice World, the skating rink my father owned and operated in Totowa, New Jersey. When coaching, practicing, or playing, I often felt that I was truly in "the zone," although I didn't call it that. In fact, I didn't give it a name at all. I just knew I felt free when engaged in athletics, and that freedom felt right—it still does.

While in college, I mentored underprivileged kids through a community service program sponsored by my school, Hamilton College. Once again, my level of well-being while mentoring and coaching always seemed to be extremely high. I experienced the game, the rink, and life in general with a degree of confidence and ease that comes from knowing I was in the proper place at the proper time. When we're young, we don't second-guess or overanalyze this type of feeling; we just know it is natural, and we're right. When my playing days were over, I was asked to coach the junior varsity team at Hamilton. I jumped at the chance to start what I knew would be my life's ultimate calling.

However, not long after my college years were behind me, I took a detour—not one based on my own gut feeling or passion. For a time, I bought into the notion that coaching couldn't be my "serious" career and that it was time to be an adult and stop dreaming. That detour took me into the business world and, ultimately, to the field of residential construction. I worked hard and did well, although truthfully, working in construction never felt quite right, not like the "comfort-zone" days of playing, mentoring, and coaching. As a result, errant thoughts, feelings, and, at times, decisions became all too common.

Along the way, I did make a smart choice: I married the love of my life, and we now have three active teenagers who keep us running. What kept me in the game (and sane) during these "detour years," literally and figuratively, was the joy I found in coaching my kids' sports teams. Later, I welcomed the opportunity to coach high school athletes. In that arena, I found a level of well-being where clarity and perspective ruled, no matter what apparent issues occurred. What does a high level of well-being produce? Productive decisions and behaviors, successful teams with eager players, and the ability to see, in the moment, the big picture of life and impart this wisdom to players you care about.

So, what was missing? First, I knew in a nagging kind of way that I wasn't pursuing my career dream, an instinct that flowed out of a natural aptitude for coaching and the sensations it gave back to me. Second, I was intensely curious about the source of the inner peace I found when working with players. I wondered, *Is it actually the process of coaching or an understanding inside of me that conjures up clarity at certain times?*

About fifteen years ago, this wonder prompted a journey that led me to the consulting offices of Pransky & Associates in La Conner, Washington. There, I met George Pransky and Keith Blevens, and later Aaron Turner, Nikki Nieves, and Mara Gleason. I learned about the work of Sydney Banks, which revolves around the innate principles of mind, consciousness, and thought as well as their function in determining how life is truly experienced. In turn, my understanding of these principles led me to create Inner Sports and later to write this book.

Now, when the conversation turns to principles such as mind, consciousness, and thought, some people scratch their heads and flash me a puzzled look. Isn't that the complicated stuff of scholars, philosophers, or Zen masters? The answer is *no*. Because our experience and the quality of our lives—not just day to day, but moment to moment—depend entirely on our level of consciousness. It might sound intricate, but in reality, it's revolutionarily simple.

Our state of consciousness determines if our view of the outside world is cloudy or clear, and over the years this profound principle has been described in many different ways. *State of mind, mood, well-being, awareness,* and *level of psychological functioning* are the words and phrases that I often interchange. Actually, the principle of consciousness is not such a mystery. Our thoughts and senses tell us all we need to know about it. In terms of sports, it's how we feel during a game we're playing, coaching, or watching; the way we respond to what looks like a mistake or an achievement; or the way we define a loss or a win.

How do thought and the inner world of mind and consciousness influence playing, coaching, or even parenting an athlete? Everyone can point to situations where fear got in the way of shooting a free throw, anxious thoughts led to a fumbled ball, or reacting in the moment contributed to a poor coaching or parenting decision. As coaches or parents, isn't it our job to teach something to counter these "bad" outcomes? Aren't we supposed to train players to come through in the clutch or focus on the trophy at the end of the season? Isn't there something here to make right? The answer again is no.

Although many talk about the mental side of sports, that phrase includes a myriad of interpretations and, unfortunately, often has little to do with mind, consciousness, and thought. These principles have hardly made their way into the athletic coaching arena at all. In fact, many coaches dutifully follow the path of conventional thinking, attacking the so-called mental game by revving up the brains and bodies of their players. They are advocates for the adrenaline-spiking pep talk used for generations and believed to be the answer to preparing for a competition. Some coaches, especially those in individual sports like tennis, golf, or gymnastics, even combine this revved-up chatter with a host of relaxation tools. Perhaps they've been taught that there's value in *trying* to visualize the flight of the ball or in picturing a gold medal.

In this book, I reveal the truth: Revving up a player serves to bind performance rather than enhance it. It always leads to errant decisions and, thus, results in missed opportunities and poor performances. By the same token, calming techniques like deep breathing often turn into a pass-fail test of how relaxed the athlete can become, and for what purpose? The truth is, sometimes we succeed when employing deep-breathing techniques, and sometimes we don't.

By using these preparation tools to pump themselves up or calm themselves down, coaches and athletes learn to rely on external factors to regulate their internal thoughts and feelings. They begin to believe that their performance, a win or a loss, is dependent on how revved up or relaxed they can be. What happens, then, if circumstances change and the team has to take to the ice, the field, or the court without the pep talk? What happens if our level of well-being in the moment prevents the visualization? What happens to players who believe there is some tool or system to master and they haven't found it yet? Regrettably, a mentality exists within athletics (and many other fields) that leads players and coaches to embark on a search for a technique or a theoretical model, or even illicit behavior, that will unearth the secret to success.

Yes, improving skills through training and practice is fundamental for achievement. Beyond that, however, no external mental tool, system, or model actually exists that will help you find long-term success or personal contentment. To the contrary, once you understand that as human beings we form our perceptions from the inside out, that the quality of our thinking and level of awareness move up and down independent of our circumstances, you will see that it makes little sense to work yourself through a temporarily low state of mind. You will also see that, left alone, the human mind will instinctively self-correct to clarity and consciousness.

• • •

The following chapters contain numerous examples of this new and revolutionarily simple paradigm. This book will show you why the sports world has lost its way and how stillpower, and not willpower, can get anyone back on track. As you read, consider your own successes and failures, your own dreams and fears; notice that effort, achievement, and life aren't supposed to be so complicated. *Stillpower* is designed to point you in a different direction than just about every other psychology or performance book on the market today. It is not meant to dictate behavior. This book's purpose is to allow your own insights and freedom to flourish.

You are about to discover that there is a different approach available in sports—and in life. Therefore, I am inviting you to approach this book differently. For the time being, put aside all the how-to methodologies of the self-help world—what you have been taught about competitive states of mind, hard work, and the true path to winning performances, titles, or medals. This is your chance to expand your level of understanding and see that beyond the intellect, there's nothing you must learn, or even do, in order to get the most out of coaching, training, or playing the game.

For the truth is this: *You already know.*

1

THE MISCONCEPTION: ATHLETICS TEACH LIFE LESSONS

*It was always fun for me. I loved baseball
so darn much. By the hours I practiced,
you'd have to say that I was really working,
but it was pretty much tireless fun.*
Ted Williams

We hear it all the time (and many of us even believe it most of the time): Playing sports is a great way to learn about life. Or, sports teach life lessons. Problem is, in the world of high school, collegiate, or professional sports today, a multitude of players seem to be leading troubled lives. While the predicaments of numerous well-known athletes might seem severe, many are examples of individuals who most of us believed had mastered an understanding of life, just because they had mastered an understanding of how to play a sport.

Quite frankly, we have the whole relationship backwards. An individual cannot learn how to compete, be resilient, or lead through sports—and then seamlessly apply these lessons to his or her life. It is possible, however, for an individual to understand what life is truly about and then apply that wisdom to the sport that he or she plays. Tiger Woods, for instance, clearly trained his entire life to be a world-class athlete, a player with integrity. Yet, in 2009, we all saw that he had failed to apply this training to his life away from the golf course.

Like the athletes and coaches I work with, I grew up in the world of sports. My father was a gritty competitor on the field and probably the best hockey coach I have ever seen in action. He ran a skating rink, so I naturally developed an aptitude for coaching ice hockey by watching him, later becoming a successful coach in my own right. But, all the while, I was struggling in my personal life. I constantly wondered why I couldn't apply the same sense of peace I found at the rink or when sitting privately with a player to other life encounters. Fortunately (as discussed in the introduction to this book), this apparent quandary led me to answers that changed my life: I was introduced to the principles of mind, consciousness, and thought. With this new understanding, I found contentment away from my comfort zone of working with athletes and I actually became a better coach. Today, as I delve deeper into these principles, my day-to-day ease in my coaching business and in all aspects of my life continues to grow.

Virtually every day, a parent says to me something like, "My daughter is struggling with teamwork, discipline, and confidence, so I'm going to get her involved in sports." Contrary to popular opinion, though, playing sports will not automatically boost a child's self-worth, teach teamwork, or instill discipline. Yes, we all yearn for an understanding of the principles that lead to contentment and success. Yet sports alone will not provide a crash course in these principles, and if you try to force it, I promise the results will be fleeting at best.

In the United States today, young people are involved in athletics more than ever before. According to the National Youth Sports Council, more than fifty million American boys and girls under the age of eighteen participate in some form of organized sporting activity. Looking just at high school participation, there are over seven million boys and girls playing one or more sports.[1] These numbers, and the future development of the impressionable participants, explain why we should not hinder, even innocently, the natural instincts of our young athletes.

The truth is, adults often forget that if not for us, kids would play sports simply for the natural joy they bring. We don't need to tell them what they're going to learn or what's important once they are immersed in the process. Kids will naturally gravitate toward what excites them, and in that arena, they will compete with maximum effort and openness, if left to their own devices. Now, please don't misunderstand me—I am not saying our young athletes do not require quality coaching and guidance. It's just that most coaches, teachers, and parents today overlook the following key motivator: children yearn to produce, not to consume.

Unlike in most of their school activities (and this is unfortunate), through sports kids discover the magical process of training and putting the preparation through a practical application, adjusting moment to moment and seeing where the chips ultimately fall. They grow by learning to sense the rhythm of the game or the journey, and by trusting themselves and their teammates. They progress by developing the ability to lead and the patience to listen.

It is, therefore, important for coaches and parents to understand that while they obviously have a major role here, that role revolves around *allowing* this process to unfold. Forcing effort, judging behavior, or trying to mold players potentially thwarts creativity and, ultimately, stifles free will. What all children (and adults, too) are looking for is an unbounded environment where they are permitted to follow their passions, express themselves fully, and compete in absence of the fear of failure.

Performance Coaching: What's Wrong with Current Thinking?

Simplicity, creativity, and passion are among the main themes of this book. In fact, I have never worked with a player who was not initially attracted to this perspective. For example, some time ago I spent several productive days working with a professional athlete who had developed the habit of bouncing from performance coach to sports psychologist and back again in search of a way to make the athletic journey more enjoyable and successful. I call it a habit because that's what it had become. It seemed to me that this player was innocently using his time with these specialists as a crutch: a way to unburden himself and perhaps pick up a technique that might help him play better, temporarily, the next night. Problem was, internally he was struggling, and externally he was mired in a scoring slump. A teammate of his, who is a client of mine, suggested that I might be able to help him put an end to his exhausting external search. He was right and as you will see, I learned a lot through my association with this player as well.

What occurred to me during our time together is that the following flaw is present in the methodology of 99 percent of the coaches, performance experts, and PhDs who are employed by teams, work privately with athletes, or generously volunteer their time: they do not understand the meaning of stillpower. That is, when an athlete is at his or her best, the experience is one of clarity and ease. Yet these so-called experts keep providing external tools and techniques that only rev up, cloud, and bind the thinking of the very individuals who they are trying to help.

Why is this happening? Because, unfortunately, "pop" psychology has convinced these experts that an athlete's life experience, or his performance on the field, is the source of his state of mind. While just the opposite is the case—an athlete's state of mind is the source of his life experience, and thus his performance.[2] And until coaches and performance experts grasp this understanding, responsiveness, stability, and inner peace will elude the sports world. Plus, players who exist at the mercy of these external approaches will continue to struggle more than ever.

Three Paths to Consistency—You Choose

Players struggle because, inadvertently, these approaches are complicating a straightforward process. I believe that once an individual notices a psychological issue hindering performance, he has three possible options or paths at his disposal.

Option One: The athlete can merely wait and hope that the errant thoughts, feelings, and performance issues will eventually subside. This solution is akin to driving around with your car's engine warning light on and not understanding what the light actually means. The light (your feelings) isn't normal, but you tell yourself that it's no big deal and try to ignore it. For some reason, however, as you try not to focus on it, your thoughts are drawn more and more to the dashboard and the incessant flashing. In fact, you have a hard time escaping it.

Option Two: The same warning light appears, but this time you know it means that something is wrong with the engine. Since you don't know exactly what the apparent problem is or how to fix it, you take the car to a mechanic. The mechanic has all sorts of tools and techniques and fixes the issue. You drive away and the car runs fine—for a few days. Then the light returns, and the same or another issue crops up again. Because you decide that the previous mechanic must not have the right technique, you search for another mechanic who has a different bag of external answers, and then another, and another. This example sadly represents the current state of performance coaching in athletics today.

Option Three: Here is an entirely new approach. You find a mechanic who can teach you the inner workings of the engine. Once you uncover the innate principles that power it, you realize that this knowledge will always be at your disposal, allowing you to diagnose and adjust effortlessly, maintaining optimal engine performance. When the warning light comes on the next time, you can simply look inward to find the answer.

With option one, the player is perplexed by his lack of consistency and is powerless to address it. With option two, the player looks "out there" for a fix, and thus the cycle from one external solution to the next begins. With option three, however, the player learns to understand

and subsequently uncover the secrets to consistent performance for himself.

The Misalignment Between the Experiences of Athletes and the Strategies of Coaches

Over the past decade, I have interviewed hundreds of world-class athletes regarding their thoughts and feelings about great play and poor play. They describe *high performance* as "freedom," "natural," "easy," "comes out of nowhere," and "requires no thought." They define *low performance* as "bound up," "work," "trying," "cluttered," and "overthinking."

This being the case, why do practically all professional teams promote mind-bending and unnatural mental-conditioning methods (option number two in the previous section) that ultimately lead to low levels of performance? Let's look at one such method: the preshot ritual. When sticking to a defined routine before a foul shot in basketball, players report that sometimes they work so hard to remember the routine that they miss, and other times they make shot after shot without even thinking about the routine. A player's performance, I believe, should never hinge on the temporary relief of coping strategies such as affirmations, imagery, or prescribed habits. In athletics, sometimes we win, sometimes we lose, but in either case the opportunity always exists for growth and future achievement.

The sports world is making success far more difficult than it is meant to be. The only answer to enduring performance, and internal contentment, lies within an innate understanding that we all possess and that the outside world (like those experts) shrouds. A player's experience—happiness, sadness, success, or failure—results from his or her thinking, ensuing feelings, and level of well-being in the moment. When an athlete is suffering, the worst thing he or she can do is search for a fix. Coaches or performance gurus who persuade their players to alter behavior based on temporary triumphs or failures are encouraging them to become passive victims of life itself. They're focusing on impermanent outcomes as opposed to the normal flow of mental health. From this viewpoint, it's easy to see why so many athletes believe the path to accomplishment rests in a mental exercise, a theoretical tool, psychotherapy, cheating, or even a pill.[3]

Do you remember the professional athlete who liked to bounce from one performance expert to another? Well, lucky for both of us, he was at the end of his rope with the "technique-of-the-week methodology." After we talked for a while, he peacefully said, "Coach, I'm at my best when I don't think, or better yet, when my thoughts come from God. Does that make sense?" Now, I am not a religious person, but I thought, *How cool is this?* From a moment of clarity and quiet, he was describing the intrinsic level of psychological functioning from which great play is truly born. He was describing stillpower.

At that very moment, I realized this player would be well on his way to uncovering a new outlook on the path of his career. I also felt then, and continue to believe now, that it is incumbent on my colleagues and me to keep writing and speaking about these types of encounters. Our responsibility is to initiate a paradigm shift both in the arena of athletic performance and in the environments that allow each player, coach, and parent to exist at the highest possible level of psychological functioning.

2

UNBOUNDED EFFORT, WILLPOWER, AND INSIGHT

*What the inner voice says will not
disappoint the hoping soul.*
FRIEDRICH SCHILLER

Not long ago, I spent a splendid Saturday afternoon at my son's high school baseball game. It was a beautiful spring day, and moods, including mine, were high all around. At this particular school, a running track encircles the field and, to my delight, another high-spirited individual made an appearance that day. He was a dark-haired boy, about five years of age, who decided that a run around the track might be fun. He ran one full lap, then another, and then about three more. Grinning ear to ear, he maintained his pace, and when he finally stopped running, it wasn't because he was tired. Like the rest of us at the game, he'd heard the bells, recognized the sound and, in a flash, he took off for the ice cream truck. No one told this youngster to run, no one was timing his laps, and no tangible goal was in sight. He didn't even appear conscious of anyone watching him. His big smile, however, told me all I needed to know about his feelings in the moment: He was demonstrating the natural impulse of what I call *unbounded effort.*

But what if we hit the fast-forward button and look at this same child a few years later? Will we find him in a football huddle gritting his teeth and clenching his jaw? Will he be enduring a lecture from a parent or coach about the benefits of hard work? Maybe we'll see someone standing on the sideline with a stopwatch, a grim face, and a mountain of expectations. Despite these likely circumstances, I hope we see him gravitating toward the feeling he had that day of his run, that boundless freedom available in all athletic endeavors and in life as well.

You've probably heard this common coaching catchphrase: The only thing that an athlete has total control over is his or her effort. Who can argue with the concept? After all, it has a certain logic to it. We can't ask more or less of players than to try their hardest. To be honest, I once firmly believed in this message myself and applied it as a coach. This message, however, misses one of the central points of this book: The more we try to control our effort (or our thoughts about effort), the more we tend to get in our own way—and reduce our odds for success. Instead, if athletes and coaches want to get the most out of training, practicing, or playing the game, they need to recall the same joy the little boy produced when he ran around the track that spring day. When effort is unbounded, we don't even think about trying hard.

What happens when we don't think about trying hard? We experience higher levels of performance, pure unabashed enjoyment, and a powerful little experience called "the zone."

What Is the Zone?

We often hear it from successful athletes at the conclusion of an awesome contest, usually in an attempt to make sense of a performance they cannot explain: "I don't know," they'll say, "I was just in the zone today."

The zone—that magical, timeless, peaceful place that spawns great play.

While many athletes recognize what it means to be in the zone, I'm not sure that I've ever heard it clearly defined. So, let me take a shot by stating that, unlike many coaches, to me the zone is *not* some heightened state of focus or concentration. The zone is the heavenly place where external limitations cease to exist. It's sort of an invisible thing—more of a feeling, really, an experience. And since describing a feeling or experience is like trying to explain the unexplainable, let us continue the discussion by describing in greater detail what the zone is not.

The zone is not the intellect. When athletes are in the zone, they exist purely in the present, with minimal thinking or analyzing. In the heat of the moment, NFL quarterbacks, for example, must somehow integrate their field position; the location of their receivers; and the distance, speed, and trajectory with which to throw the ball. Not to mention the three-hundred-pound linemen bearing down on them.

These quarterbacks operate with a level of precision that belies their lack of intellectual analysis. True, football is a game involving geometry and physics, but when they are on top of their game, these athletes are not consciously making calculations. In fact, they're barely thinking about anything at all. Almost magically, the field unfolds before them, they see their options, and they simply react and throw. And more times than not, they find their target successfully.

It is also clear to me that the zone is not about trying hard. When in the zone, there is no conscious effort or grind. The zone feels simple, unbounded, and easy. Time seems to slow; options look obvious. Although athletes in the zone are incredibly locked in, this focus is never forced. These players are experiencing such clarity and vision that focus becomes a mere afterthought.

The word most synonymous with the notion of the zone, to me, is *freedom*. When athletes play with freedom, they don't think; they know. They don't focus; they feel. They don't grind; they allow. This means that an individual is performing with a complete understanding that external circumstances (linemen bearing down, overbearing parents, perceived pressure from coaches) have no ability to regulate his or her life. From here, an athlete is operating at the height of consciousness with his perceptual field wide open. Everything is seen as an asset; no matter what occurs, the player cannot fail. In the freedom and connectivity of the zone, external limitations cease to exist.

Finding that Magical Mind-Set

This freedom, this connection to the game, this experience of unbounded effort is what we love about playing sports in the first place. Every athlete, at some point in his or her career, experiences this pure presence. Some athletes, however, experience the zone more often than others, leading to consistency and higher levels of performance. And although the manner of reaching this state of mind varies from athlete to athlete, the potential within all of us for finding it is exactly the same.

So, how do the great ones do it? This might sound strange, but they don't *try* to do anything.

Once an individual believes there is something he must do in order to find the zone, he is lost before he starts. I have often overheard coaches instructing players to be more intense, to focus, or to concentrate—only to watch the performances of those players go straight downhill. I have also spoken to many athletes who say that on days when they aren't in the zone, they try so hard to get there that they eventually trip over their own two feet.

Again, the only way to find this entirely instinctual state of mind is to understand that there is no act required on your part. When children are upset, they don't use a technique, strategy, or mantra in order to return to contentment—it happens by design. Reflect for a second on the best performances or purest experiences in your own life. Were you trying to exert willpower, or force it, when you found yourself in this fulfilling place?

What many players have told me is that they find the zone when they refuse to force it. Without a deliberation, they are able to let go. They let go of performance expectations and external thoughts of stress or nervousness and just absorb themselves into the present moment. In other words, being in the zone is a selfless experience. The more athletes think about themselves—i.e., how they're feeling, are they ready, how they look, what the fans think, what their parents think, whether they'll get pulled if they make a mistake—the less likely they find themselves playing with the unbounded effort required to enter the zone.

Let's return to the little running boy. Was he thinking? Was he trying? Was he worried about expectations? Did he care about how he looked or what anyone thought? Not at all. He was just running and playing, full of effort, full of joy—wonderfully free.

The Grind of Willpower

All too often, athletes believe there is something that they must do in order to grind themselves into the zone. They think they can will themselves into this level of mental functioning. And in the absence of a better solution, external sources have convinced them that willpower will help get them there. But it simply won't work.

I would argue that using willpower is the exact opposite of unbounded effort, the exact opposite of playing in the zone. Sadly, it seems that most of the athletes I work with believe, at first, that willpower is a positive attribute and often ask me to help them develop more. Willpower, though, is not as powerful as popular culture would have us believe, especially over the long term.

I am about to propose a fundamental departure from the mainstream thinking that we need willpower to succeed. This idea, blamelessly propagated by coaches, parents, and the media, is hampering the performance of athletes and coaches worldwide. In fact, athletes who carry the continuous burden of mustering up willpower rank among the most inconsistent and frustrated players who walk into my office.

To help clarify, I recently watched a TV commercial for a weight-loss company. The company claimed to help clients develop the willpower to eat less. I also heard a basketball coach describe his players' tendency to commit fouls under pressure and his plan to increase their willpower at crunch time. Yet, while the weight-loss company might help you conjure up the courage to lose a few pounds, and while the coach might help his team overcome its unruly play for one night, using willpower to combat these habits will only have so much staying power. In most cases, the weight will return and the players will revert to their previous level of performance.

This is because willpower requires forced power over one's will—synonymous with battling one's own thinking or state of mind. This belief implies that a person hasn't had a true change of heart, hasn't let go. Yes, according to most dictionaries, *willpower* is defined as "the strength of will to carry out one's decisions, wishes, or plans." But this definition is incorrect in its assumption that strength of will—or clashing with one's own thoughts—can actually help individuals to execute their plans successfully. We are productive, and thus successful, when we apply *free will*, not *strength of will*, to a project of any kind. Free will allows us to adjust and imagine. It prevents us from getting in our own way as we create the appropriate path for ourselves *in spite* of our preconceived decisions, wishes, or plans.

Willpower might help an athlete get off the couch to go for a training run. It might help another choose a salad and whole-grain pasta over a hamburger and French fries. But it won't help an athlete find the zone, and it certainly won't lead to unbounded effort. Over the long haul, contentment and great play spring from the clarity, quiet, and freedom of the zone—i.e., stillpower—and *not* from force or strength.

There is one more thing to consider about willpower. If willpower is required to push you through a performance, then I wonder: Are you truly passionate about what you are doing in the first place? Once again, think of any performance in your life when you were at your best. Did you need strength of will to get you in the game? Can you define what really carried you along?

Insight versus Strength of Will

I once posed the following question to a professional hockey player who was a big believer in willpower: "On days when you are a little lost out on the ice and use your strength of will to find yourself, how exactly do you accomplish this?" The player responded with the example of how a recent game started out poorly because he felt that he and his linemates weren't focused. Upon this realization, he said to his linemates, "Stop worrying about concentrating. The goalie [on the opposing team] is leaving the top right corner of the net wide open, so let's skate our butts off and keep shooting at that corner." Feeling full of energy, he proceeded to score two key goals in his team's victory. He insisted it was his own strength of will that averted a bad game and the possibility of a prolonged slump in performance.

What this player failed to distinguish, however, was that the turnaround was the result of a personal revelation, not the result of trying hard. In fact, he later told me that while his linemates were attempting to ratchet up intensity, it intuitively occurred to him, *I've got nothing to lose, so why not hustle as if there's no tomorrow and shoot high right?* In spite of appearances to the contrary, insight—and not strength of will—paved the way to a heightened (and freeing) effort level and to his subsequently winning performance.

Insight is infinitely more powerful than willpower. Actually, insight, or having a new idea and/or a change of heart, erases the need for strength or force of will of any kind.

Another client, a basketball player, once told me he gets so uptight before games that he can barely sleep or eat and rarely feels "right." He asked me how he should deal with these "awful feelings" because he claimed that, by the time he gets to the arena, his energy is pretty much sapped by all the mental processing that's been going on in the hours leading up to the game. Well, I was definitely sympathetic to this player's feelings of dread. But my first order of business in this type of situation is to help a player understand the source of his feelings, the reason for the lack of an insightful solution, and why he is compounding the apparent problem. Essentially, nervousness has no power whatsoever to sap a player's energy—it's just nervousness. And the more an athlete tries to will the feelings away, the worse things will become.

This athlete, however, couldn't see that the idea of nervousness thwarting performance was merely an innocent thought and nothing to worry about. Perhaps a coach had once told him, "You better calm down or you won't have any energy left to play," or maybe he just assumed that because nervousness didn't feel good to him that it represented a barrier to success.

The sensation of nervousness, believe it or not, is neutral. In terms of performance, it might help. It might hurt. Or it might not have much impact at all. Glenn Hall, a storied NHL goaltender, used to throw up before every single game of his professional career.[1] Yet he was voted into thirteen all-star games as well as the Hockey Hall of Fame. Clearly, nervousness was not a barrier to Glenn Hall's optimum performance. He was able to roll with it and find his own way to embrace the feeling. He understood that his nervousness was present for a reason and would fade away once the game began.

Now to the question of what the basketball player should have done with the pit in his stomach and the nervous thoughts at its source. The only effective answer is: Just let them be. If allowed, they will clear up on their own. Whenever an athlete, or any person, judges his own thoughts and feelings, he will always be inclined to counteract them. And once he tries, the more his thinking will rev up and the more his stomach will churn. Simply recognizing that we create our own realities via our own thoughts (such as believing nerves alter performance) will ultimately serve to render the feelings powerless.

As a matter of fact, at first this basketball player wondered why I didn't offer a behavioral tool or recommend willpower to help him feel and perform better. Then a powerful insight occurred to him. He envisioned that his nervousness had no ability to bring him down and would soon wither away on its own, only to be replaced with sensations of positivity and enthusiasm. It was a sure sign that he was headed in the right direction to achieving a consistent and contented level of performance.

The Zone and Willpower: A Final Thought

For those of you who are now uncertain about what it takes to succeed on the field, court, course, or ice, here is my final question on the subject of willpower: If struggles only occur when an individual is not operating from a clear mind-set, then why do so many of us attempt to figure things out from this muddled mental state?

The answer, as we have just seen, is to do precisely the opposite. Simply quiet down and contrast the feeling of willpower with the feelings of stillpower: ease, clarity, and responsiveness. It will then become obvious that buying into the outer world's definition of "how we overcome" (focus, might, and willpower) will not help you find the solutions to roadblocks, shaky starts, or inconsistent play. Sure, hustling your butt off and shooting for the open corner may be the way out if you're a hockey player and you're underperforming in the moment. But you can only be certain that this notion is the right one for the long haul and, for your greater life, if it comes from the ease of an insight and not from the force of your intellect or will.

At the risk of touching on the spiritual side of sports, to all athletes who are out there searching and striving for an unbounded level of psychological functioning, my heartfelt suggestion is to stop—right now. Your search is leading you farther away from what you seek. The zone exists in the depths of every person's soul. It is athletics' version of *Truth* or even *Spirit*, a level of awareness where all is right in the world, and the game and life just flow. While I know that my words have failed to do this state of mind justice, I hope that the feeling of freedom and unbounded effort revealed in this chapter is enough to give all athletes a glimpse of the zone's capabilities— and what they must understand, and *not* do, in order to find it.

3

COACHING, WISDOM, AND SUCCESS

I may not be the lion,
but it was left to me to give the lion's roar.
WINSTON CHURCHILL

In the opening chapter, I discussed the misconception that sports participation always leads to learned (and retained) life lessons. In this chapter, we'll look at a contributing factor to this misconception: a lack of understanding by coaches (teachers and parents as well) of the all-important principle of their own state of mind. While you might already be able to tell that an athlete's state of mind is a hot topic with me, rarely, if ever, are this principle and coaching thought of collectively.

To be clear, I applaud and respect anyone who possesses the will to mentor another human being and, from my standpoint, 99 percent of our coaches take on the job for the proper reasons. However, most of these individuals are not getting through to their players or students, and if they are, the proper lessons are not being taught.

So let's spell out this overlooked but indispensable ingredient to successful coaching or leadership: A coach must, in the moment, be more grounded in a level of mental functioning than his or her player. Yet every day coaches are drilling, instructing, or counseling when they are not in the right mind-set to do so. Put another way: What you say to your player is far less important than your state of mind when you say it. To effectively engage someone, you must be operating from a higher level of consciousness than the other person at that moment. I often advise coaches that this understanding supersedes any other requirement if they are to provide enduring guidance, recommendations, or love.

Several years ago, a seventeen-year-old equestrian and his mother made an appointment to see me. While sitting in my office, the young man became extremely distraught and proceeded to lament the pressure he felt his parents had applied over the years. Then, right in front of me, the mother actually chastised the boy for not being tough enough. As you can imagine, all kinds of negative thoughts about this parent flooded through my head. I decided, however, to put my thinking aside and hang in there. With an attentive and clear mind, I listened to this young athlete, and his mother, and offered a small dose of heartfelt advice. Afterwards, when we said our good-byes, I wasn't sure if my words had made a lasting impact, but at least both mother and son were calm. Then, about three hours later, the woman called and repeatedly thanked me for my sound guidance and message. She said that, on the way home, the two of them had their first real conversation in years.

Now that call really caught me off guard and, at the same time, taught me a valuable lesson. In contrast to other moments in my coaching career when I tried so hard to instill a message and it went right over the other person's head, all I had really done this time was listen (and make minimal suggestions) from a higher level of mental functioning than my clients possessed at that time. In fact, it is now clear that when I become overly passionate or lose my bearings in any way, it is nearly impossible for me to get a point across, no matter how educated the message might be.

This illustration reveals an issue that confronts coaches, teachers, or mentors of any kind. Our athletes, students, and children need leaders who understand the power of their own level of psychological functioning and the impact that it has on the world outside. You cannot give a player a twenty-dollar bill if you only have a five in your pocket. So, the next time you feel the urge to provide guidance or discipline, please understand that what comes out of your mouth is much less significant than the level of mental functioning from which the words are spoken.

Love and Coaching

When I talk about mental functioning, I mean your mood, your state of mind, your level of psychological aptitude in the moment. The most important thing that we can do as coaches, I think, is interact with our players from a state of mind brimming with love, compassion, and selflessness. It's not our words, but the *feeling* behind our words, that will make a difference.

One significant stumbling block to this understanding, though, is that individuals who are immersed in the world of athletics rarely use the word *love* when talking about the attributes essential to becoming a proficient coach. I would argue that love may well be number one on the list. Without love for your players, the game, or life itself, it is impossible to value the journey of a season and view the so-called ups and downs with clarity. For example, when Duke University basketball coach Mike Krzyzewski faces a setback or wonders why he puts himself through the daily rigors of college basketball, he calmly tells himself, "It must be love." And while love may not always seem to make sense or be convenient in the moment, because love requires fluent thinking and thus a heightened level of consciousness, it always carries Krzyzewski through.[1]

Sadly, many coaches make the mistake of indulging the challenging thoughts and feelings that appear to be byproducts of external situations: handling a tough loss, working with a temperamental player, or facing a difficult opponent. From this blurred state of mind, they react and make decisions that often magnify the perceived negative situation. Suddenly, the reasons they are there in the first place (the joy, excitement, and lessons to teach) become lost, and all too often coaches find themselves alone on an island facing the criticism of fans, the press, or even parents.

If you as a coach, or any type of teacher for that matter, want to uncover the true meaning of helping others, then follow the advice of one of my favorite authors, Alan Cohen, who once said, simply, "Keep loving."[2] External how-to resources are not at all necessary; love will provide all the direction that you seek. With love as your guide, you will find solace in the process and appreciate the bumps in the road as you impart wisdom to your players, opponents, and fellow coaches. From this instinctive place of freedom in action, you will become more competitive and successful; the game and life will flow naturally—without complication.

. . .

There is one other applicable and often overlooked definition of the word *love* that I want to mention here. Author and lecturer Wayne Dyer once said, "Love is the ability and willingness to allow those whom you care for to be what they choose for themselves without any insistence that they satisfy you."[3] All too often coaches will adopt a my-way-or-the-highway, ego-driven attitude. This narrow-mindedness impedes team and individual growth and potentially stifles a player's free will. With this attitude, clear thinking and respect will never be realized, and long-term success is nearly impossible. Great coaches—Krzyzewski, Tony Dungy, Joe Torre, Pat Summitt, Urban Meyer, C. Vivian Stringer, and John Wooden—consistently set guidelines based on one overriding principle: love for their players. From this perspective of stillpower, the right lessons will always be taught, insights always uncovered, and the true meaning of the game always found.

Developing True Team Players

Without fail, mentoring from a loving state of mind will help coaches realize long-term success and earn the respect of their players. Effortlessly, love draws out the innate wisdom and common sense that reside in all human beings. In this environment, athletes are more at ease, so they perform at a level of freedom that allows them to smoothly reach their full potential.

Indeed, drawing out others' inner knowledge is a primary requirement for any leader. But, I'm sorry to say, many uninformed coaches and teachers are doing the opposite today; they are dictating to their players or students about how to behave. While their intentions are almost always good, they are helping to create unimaginative athletes with absolutely zero individuality and ability to translate lessons to life.

Yes, all teams and organizations do need a set of guidelines and rules to be successful. But too often these boundaries are chosen because of a coach's ego-driven thoughts on how things should be run. Instead, coaches need merely to tap into their own inner wisdom and just be themselves. Then the proper parameters for their team will be established, always.

New York Giants head coach Tom Coughlin once admitted that many of the requirements he had placed on his players over the years didn't feel natural to him, but his common sense was overridden by the need to be in charge. During a quiet moment in the 2007 off-season, he decided to listen to his inner voice. He kept some of his old rules, discarded others, and in turn created an environment of cooperation and freedom for his team. The coach then earned a newfound respect among his players, and that year the Giants won the first of two Super Bowl championships under Coughlin.[4]

The lesson to be learned here is: As a coach or mentor of any kind, you have to be careful to avoid the trap of forcing your belief system on your players or students. One of my mentors, Sydney Banks, once said, "If you take a belief of your own and replace it with another's belief, you might experience a temporary placebo effect, but you have not found a lasting answer. However, if a person replaces an old belief with a realization from his or her own inner wisdom, the effect and results are superior and permanent."[5]

Any great teacher understands that when you blindly adopt another person's beliefs, you stop thinking for yourself and become a follower. My opinion is that we need more leaders, not followers.

What About the Player's Responsibilities?

Endless potential exists for coaches who understand the value in fostering the innate wisdom that rests within their athletes. A high school football coach recently told me that he now sees how this outlook can enhance ingenuity and self-reliance, thereby supporting the development of his players and the success of his team. But at the same time, he was slightly confused about how strictly he should enforce some of the rules that he felt were still necessary.

"What are a player's responsibilities?" he asked me. "Isn't it the player's obligation to follow the rules that a coach hands down, whether the rules agree with the player's beliefs or not?"

The short answer to this question is absolutely yes. But, as a coach, you must grasp the true purpose in having rules in the first place.

Rules, like laws in society, put limits on behavior for the intention of looking after the greater good. An organization must set regulations so self-rule, and thus conduct, won't run amuck. The trick, though, is to set these rules in a manner that also nurtures free will and original thinking. Specifically, a coach must explain (to his team) the purpose for setting boundaries as opposed to dictating from the ego and saying, "My way is the only way, and if you don't like it, there's the door."

Most players who participate in team sports are well aware, before they take the field, that team rules are going to be in place. Plus, odds are that a player is going to disagree from time to time with several of those rules. For team unity to be possible, however, each player must understand that the rules must be adhered to above all else. As an example, many of us get impatient when stuck in a traffic jam and worry we might be late. Nonetheless, we understand that if all tardy drivers broke the law and drove on the road's shoulder, chaos would naturally ensue.

So, to be a true team player as well as maintain the individual freedom necessary for success, an athlete must put personal agendas aside but also be aware of the reasons why this is important. In 2009, the Indianapolis Colts were undefeated with only two games remaining in the regular season when head coach Jim Caldwell pulled his starting players off the field. Quarterback Peyton Manning disagreed—he didn't want to rest for the playoffs. But he also realized that the ultimate decision was his coach's to make. If he led a revolt, the team would be risking pandemonium on the sidelines.

The final element to this collective understanding, between player and coach, is that a leader—in the sports arena or any environment—should remember to always stick to his or her own gut instincts when rules are set in place or enforced. When a coach refuses to operate from ego and insecurity, he or she becomes willing to consider that a player's perspective might indeed have some added value. Many coaches fail to recognize that the most innovative teams (companies and societies as well) actually encourage individuals to express their views respectfully. Such teams have learned that personal ownership in the greater good will foster the free will that is paramount to success.

There is a poignant scene toward the end of one of my favorite movies, *Hoosiers*.[6] In it, Coach Norman Dale draws up the play sure to clinch the state basketball championship for the underdogs from Hickory High. The players, however, insightfully disagree with their esteemed coach's strategy, and you can see it in the look on their faces. An ego-free Coach Dale then encourages them to speak up by saying, "What's the matter with you guys?" They tell him, the play is changed, and Jimmy Chitwood nails the final shot. Hickory High wins the state title!

The Unknown Secret to Engaging Your Team

Hoosiers dramatically reveals what I believe to be the unknown secret to engaging your team. In short, it is never up to the coach. Engagement occurs on an individual level; it can't be commanded. Hickory High was victorious because Chitwood, his teammates, and Coach Dale were all engaged, worked in harmony, and took personal responsibility for the team's performance. They created an environment for clear-thinking play and successful coaching—promoting structure and freedom simultaneously. In this environment, coaches realize that judging or dictating behavior only helps to produce followers who are incapable of finding the courage to stand up and produce at crunch time. Players realize that, while external circumstances have no ability to alter their own belief systems, adhering to team rules (or societal laws) is an indispensable ingredient to group and individual achievement.

Yet in today's pro sports world—and this tendency trickles down to all levels—almost all coaches believe the opposite is true. We often hear that the coaches are the ones with a wealth of experience—and their necks are on the line—so they need to find a way to get the players to listen, care, and play hard. For example, say an NFL team is 5–8 and clearly out of the playoff picture with three games remaining in the season. The coach calls a team meeting with the hope of somehow motivating his players, even though it looks to everyone, including the coach, that they have nothing to play for. If the coach actually thinks he has the power to make the team believe that the last three games do mean something, he is mistaken. Everyone knows the season is over in three weeks. So then, what should the coach do? Part of his job is to have his guys ready to play every game of the season.

The coach, first and foremost, should recognize that he only possesses the ability to regulate his own engagement or passion level; he can't do anything about a losing record or the fact that the season ends in three weeks. But he can show the team that these external conditions cannot foil his passion. Once the coach becomes passionate, it becomes possible to hold his players accountable to the same standard. Regardless of external circumstances, he has then crafted an environment that is ripe for a productive pep talk and a competitive end to the season.

So coaches, here's the bottom line: In spite of what you may have been taught, true leadership never revolves around motivating your players. True leadership means showing your players that the ability to be motivated rests within each of them individually and, thus, the team collectively.

Engagement, Determination, and Compulsion

What we've been talking about is a drastically different take on leadership and a new understanding of what makes for positive and respectful player-coach relationships. Regardless of the subject matter, the often overlooked key to successful team meetings, strategy sessions, or any type of motivational talk between player and coach is that all individuals have *within them* the power to be more passionate and engaged. In fact, you might be surprised to learn that today's most innovative teams and companies hold players or employees accountable to this very understanding, hence creating a healthy, positive, and efficient culture.

Disturbingly, however, many coaches and teachers try to ramp up intensity for their players and students, rather than fostering the engagement and determination that resides within them. Among other things, this dangerous tendency wrongly encourages already busy athletes to pour even more determination and commitment into their sporting endeavors—for little gain.

Today, this trend is a common concern of athletes of all ages, and parents, too. That's why I want to close this chapter by stressing to coaches that, in particular instances, I believe it is perfectly okay and even beneficial for a player to sit out a practice, pull back from training, or even stop pursuing an apparent goal.

You may disagree. Like most coaches, you may insist that regardless of how a player feels in the moment, his or her commitment to the team must be the overriding factor. That player must find a way to grind out determination, no matter what. I appreciate where you are coming from. Still, I think you're off track, and here's the reason.

Although I consider determination to be a crucial factor for success, for us to find the freedom necessary to reach our full potential, we must first clarify the definition of determination and then learn what it truly feels like. True determination is empowering. When we are determined, we are enthusiastic, energetic, and imaginative. Determination is the opposite of compulsion; it can never be forced. When we feel the compulsion to perform a task, we will simply get in our own way, our bodies will be more prone to break down, and as many parents who push their kids to participate in certain activities know, we will never improve.

According to Alan Cohen, the challenge for all of us is to recognize the difference between inner guidance and outer thoughts of limitation (and to hold ourselves accountable to this recognition).[7] Or, from my perspective, while you were born to be determined, you were not born to be obstinate. Even determined players, coaches, or employers sometimes recognize the wisdom in pulling back, and this awareness is a far cry from quitting. To illustrate, many successful collegiate and pro coaches will, when they see their players struggling at a practice or training session, cut the gathering short and set out on a team excursion to a bowling alley, billiard hall, or movie theater. These coaches understand that players will only compound mistakes and, in the end, be less competitive, if they stubbornly plug away at it.

In other words, these coaches know that the only worth in a negative feeling, or struggle, is to notify an individual that he is about to head off course. What often separates consistent coaches from those with sporadic records is the recognition that determination and inner guidance will always feel right; compulsion or quitting, not so much. I frequently remind players and coaches that they must learn to differentiate between these two opposing gut feelings. The feeling of compulsion is a sign that, in the moment, they are looking in the wrong external direction. Determination, on the other hand, feels free and uncomplicated. This correct direction for success and personal growth is the path that leads us to answers within ourselves.

4

CLEAR THINKING, RESILIENCE, AND LIFE BEYOND THE SCOREBOARD

*There is no escaping thought—
there is only understanding.*
RICHARD CARLSON

Many successful athletes with whom I work share a common, unproductive habit. When things are going well on the field of play, I don't hear from them. When things are going poorly, they constantly touch base. While on the surface, this tendency might seem to make sense and is the accepted practice of the majority of performance coaches and sports psychologists, I believe it is unproductive on many fronts.

It is vital for an athlete to first understand that his level of well-being cannot be affected by the current state of his career. His batting average, free-throw percentage, current point streak, or even physical condition has no

47

ability to regulate his level of happiness or self-worth. The fact that a player would reach out when he is not scoring goals, for example, is a sign that insecurity or external circumstances, not intuition or inner wisdom, are running the show.

In short, an athlete's insecure thoughts will always originate from low levels of mental functioning—not from scoring slumps. So, I instruct struggling players that they don't need to work on psychological performance strategies; they need to develop an understanding of how the mind really works in the first place. Or, why turn toward the quick fix, when you can understand the inherent principles behind constructing the true groundwork for a long and successful career?

Here is the decision that players often face: Do they build a solid psychological foundation or just move around a little dirt? Falling into common external traps, such as adhering to superstition, is an example of moving dirt. Far too many athletes buy into the myth that until performance suffers—keep everything the same. Or if performance does suffer—let's change things up. To the contrary, the real secret is to continually deepen one's understanding of the principles behind performance (thought, state of mind) and, in turn, allow awareness to grow. Players with this deep understanding, this foundation, are often so absorbed in the flow of the game that not scoring doesn't look like a personal setback or problem—so no external "fix" is ever needed.

This is not to imply that a player should ever be pleased about striking out, missing an open net, or being hurt—even clear-thinking competitors tend to not take these events lightly. Yet there is a significant distinction between one's performance on the field and the quality of one's life. Until a player understands this difference, he will never live up to his potential in either department. In Arabic, for example, the word for problem is actually translated as "another view."[1] So when faced with an apparent difficulty, a player's or coach's true calling is to look inward and allow himself to uncover the source and meaning of the challenge. It is the same with apparent joys or successes. When we understand that winning also masks a deeper lesson, we see that external victories have no influence over internal contentment, and we should not be tempted by the ego's willingness to tell us otherwise.

The message is simple: Athletes and coaches who tend to look past their own thoughts (positive or negative) regarding current outcomes consistently learn, grow, and prosper—no matter what the scoreboard says. Beyond the win or loss and even the joy or sorrow, everything that occurs "out there"—every failure, every missed point, or even injury—occurs to illuminate our path, not to obscure it. Just ask Super Bowl champion quarterback Drew Brees.

What Lies Ahead if We Look Within

After the New Orleans Saints won the Super Bowl in 2010, I listened intently to all of the interviews with Drew Brees. He talked about his shoulder injury, being released from his previous team, and the pain of his arduous rehab. I practically had tears in my eyes as he spoke. I then heard him mention that when the Saints took a chance on him, he honestly didn't know if coming to New Orleans was the right move and, in the moment, he deeply questioned his faith. At this point, the Brees story really caught my interest.

Over the years, there has been plenty of news about troubled sports personalities who have suffered. Drew Brees, however, somehow knew better than to play victim to his own despairing thoughts. As a result, he found the answer to his seemingly insecure situation and created the appropriate path for himself, on and off the field. I imagine it wasn't easy, but at some point Brees looked within and realized that the solution did not rest in the quick fixes of the outside world that many athletes reach for. Relief would not be found by straying from his family, carrying a weapon to satisfy some doomed sense of self-protection, or pursuing other outside escapes or coping mechanisms. As opposed to others, Brees remained aware of one of the important messages contained in this book: The unpleasant internal feelings that accompany the desires for these types of external coping mechanisms were a sign to take a step back—not a call to action.

Let's compare Brees's post–Super Bowl interviews with another question-and-answer session in 2010, during which former New York Mets general manager and ESPN broadcaster Steve Phillips discussed his four weeks of therapy at a rehabilitation clinic in Mississippi.[2] Phillips talked about his condition, the bad choices that he made, and the pain that his actions inflicted on his family. I felt for him, his wife, and his children as I listened. Then Phillips mentioned that at the clinic, counselors discovered some unresolved pain from the past that contributed to his errant behavior. That's when the interview went south for me.

Why? Because, while I sympathized with Phillips's situation, the past is merely a thought or memory carried through time; it has no ability to regulate one's life at the current moment. Drew Brees found clarity of thought and persevered because he refused to focus on the past. A seemingly unresolved issue of yesterday has nothing to do with erroneous thinking of today. And until an individual comes to this realization, he or she will always fall prey to the conditions of life itself.

Here's what many of us ought to consider: All human beings exist, from moment to moment, at varying levels of psychological functioning. When this level of functioning is low, most often for no tangible reason, we view life through a dirty lens and are prone to deviant behavior—if we act. Once this principle is grasped, we see that navigating smoothly through life doesn't have to be so complicated, and unlike the belief of many counselors and coaches in the self-help world, it has nothing to do with personal history.

There is one other impactful principle at work in the case of Drew Brees that we should not overlook. To me, Brees represents the epitome of a creation-based thinker. Although today everyone seems to be talking about the book *The Secret*, attraction-based thinking, and the Law of Attraction, Brees understands that the ability to move forward with promise rests in one place only: himself. In spite of apparent hardships, Brees sees that the power to create the appropriate destination lies in his own attitude and actions, not in his past or anything external to him.

Sports Psychology "Control" versus the Natural Flow of Thought

In 1995, Bob Rotella became one of the first authors to talk about the principle of thought in terms of sports psychology. His highly successful and popular book *Golf Is Not a Game of Perfect* discusses how golfers can use their thinking to master the mental game of golf.

I consider Dr. Rotella to be an innovator, and I greatly respect his contributions to the field. But as I thumbed through his book, I found myself disagreeing with him about the all-important principle of thought. He wrote:

> Every now and then a player says to me something like, "Doc, I just involuntarily started thinking about hitting the ball into the water and I couldn't do anything about it." My response is, "No, you can indeed do something about it, you can think about the ball going to the target."... A golfer can and must decide how he will think.[3]

Then Rotella talked about teaching golfer Nick Price to "control his thoughts and make his game more consistent."[4]

Again, I am sorry to disagree, but the principle of thought doesn't work that way. You cannot become consistent or successful by exchanging one thought for another, deciding how to think, or trying to control thought. You can, however, navigate yourself efficiently through any competition, or life itself, by understanding what the principle of thought is in the first place.

Thought is the illusory link between what occurs in the world "out there" and the inner reality that we paint for ourselves. The quality of our thinking is constantly changing, and with it, so too are our feelings about the circumstances within a competition, such as a water hazard on a golf course. As Sydney Banks once said, "Thought is the creative agent we use to direct us through life"; a divine gift, our thinking shapes our perceptions as its quality changes moment to moment.[5]

Most performance coaches do not understand the principle of thought. They fail to see that a thought, on its own, is completely neutral (we will explore this topic in chapter 6), and no one can control what thoughts pop into his or her head. It's when we act on a thought, by attempting to suppress or replace it, that we bring it to life. Thus, golfers who try to manipulate their own thoughts will not produce consistent performance; they will only produce consistently revved-up thoughts. And while a short-term boost might be possible, long-term success from this revved-up or frenetic state of mind is impossible.

Sticking to the great game of golf, I can virtually guarantee that the most consistent performers are way too conscious to take the bait and fall victim to their own erroneous thinking. Having a thought about hitting the ball into the water or out of bounds, for instance, is neutral (and normal). Acknowledging that there is something to do about the thought makes it valid. Do you really believe that when a negative thought popped into Jack Nicklaus's head on the golf course (and yes, it happened to him, too), he said to himself, *This thought isn't a good one. I better replace it with something more positive?* Suppose, in the moment, the thought exchange failed to work. What then?

So, while I applaud Bob Rotella and others for bringing the principle of thought to the athletic arena, I believe that golf, like life, is mastered through an understanding of how thought works, not through the use of a thought-management technique. There is a big difference between understanding the principle of thought and trying to ignore, deny, or control it. Recognizing the innocent, impartial, and naturally fluent nature of your thinking is the first step toward living and performing at higher levels of well-being, day in and day out. What to do, or actually not do, when negative thinking strikes, now that's when this understanding will pay dividends, if you allow it.

Shadow Wrestling

Most of us, unfortunately, do not permit our negative thoughts to settle. We fail to realize that it is always unproductive to wage war with our own thinking in order to elevate performance levels or states of mind. In truth, fearing or trying to deal with negative thoughts only gives them *more* power. My friend and colleague Keith Blevens once told me about an old Monty Python skit in which a wrestler enters a ring and has a match against himself. In the skit, the wrestler is both champion and challenger, and obviously no one succeeds since you cannot possibly win a match with yourself. Oh, the wrestler surely tries; he pulls his own hair, twists his own leg, and grabs his own neck. But in the end, he's left right back where he started, all alone, just much worse for the wear.

While the skit is quite humorous, its message, of course, is just the opposite. Because we overlook that our thoughts and moods—and not our circumstances— create our troubles, far too many of us come to blows with a reality that we ourselves construct on a daily basis. Here's a real-life example:

Several years back, I worked with a pro running back whose usually successful football team had gotten off to an 0–3 start. He was struggling on the field, extremely disgruntled with his coach, and wanted to be traded. He did not trust the coach to lead his team to success. So, intellectually it made sense for this player to wrestle with the circumstance and either try to initiate an uprising against the coach or look for another team. This predicament resulted in many arduous planning discussions with his agent, several disagreements with his wife (who liked the city they lived in), and acrimony with his teammates. As soon as I asked the player to consider all the pressures the coach might be feeling, however, the dilemma took on a whole new appearance. Suddenly he realized that his wife was right (his family did live in a nice city), the coach was actually a "cool guy" who was struggling himself, and together they had won before—so why not this season? As the player began to understand that his thinking, thus his reality, was changing moment to moment (while his circumstances remained the same), he saw that there was no real fight to fight in the first place. In fact, with the same coach in charge, both the player and the team went on to have remarkable success the rest of that season.

What the experience of this football player reveals is that every person's reality is created via his own thinking—not by the world around him (his circumstances). And only when we grasp this understanding will we avoid "shadow wrestling" altogether. The time may come when a professional athlete decides that a trade is in his best interest; however, this choice will only be "right" if it originates from fluent thinking, never from acrimony or a struggle. Therefore, the next time a pessimistic thought invades your brain, realize there is nothing you actually need to control or even do. To paraphrase coach and author Michael Neill: Your natural state of mind is crystal clear.[6] When it becomes temporarily cloudy, similar to a murky glass of water, simply allow the sediment (your thoughts) to settle. Like a child who is temperamental one minute and gleeful the next, your mind will instinctively return to a clear level of functioning—a place where productive choices can be made and the game and life seem simple.

The Book Is Never Written

When athletes find a level of psychological functioning where the game and life flow naturally, their creative options will always expand. As opposed to the limited individual, who takes the circumstances of the outside world at face value, players and coaches who trust in the potential for their thinking to remain clear and unaffected will have access to infinite insightful solutions—especially in a decisive moment. Let's look at a situation featuring a young athlete named Jordan.

Jordan is a fine high school hockey player. As a sophomore, he has worked his way up to his school's varsity team, which is competing in the state finals. The score is 2–2 and there is 2:07 left on the clock in the championship game when the unthinkable happens. In his quest to make a big play, Jordan reaches for the puck and accidentally pulls down a player on the opposing team. The referee assesses a penalty for tripping. Jordan is in disbelief. His team now must play a man down for all but seven seconds of the remainder of the period and perhaps the game.

The coach complains, and the school's entire cheering section hurls insults at the ref: "How can you make that call at this point in the game?" "You stink, it's not about you—let the kids play!" Jordan feels awful. He believes he's let his teammates, the coach, and the entire school down. He's extremely upset as he skates to the penalty box to watch as his team tries to stop the opposition's skillful power play.

But through the hysteria, something else happens to Jordan as he arrives at the penalty box door. He realizes that if he acts from a place of anger, argues with the ref, or bangs his stick, then he might be assessed an additional penalty for unsportsmanlike conduct. His team will then be down for the first two minutes of overtime as well, if they make it that far.

While still not happy with the ref's call, Jordan sits calmly and notices something interesting. In their quest to score the decisive goal, the defensemen on the other team are both pushed up into their offensive zone. If he gets the chance, maybe, just maybe, there is an opportunity here.

Jordan watches the clock as his teammates continue to kill the penalty: twenty-five seconds left in the penalty, twenty, fifteen, ten, penalty over. There are seven seconds to go in the game, and the score is still tied 2–2. Jordan jumps out on the ice, way behind the overly eager opposing defensemen. A teammate attempts to ice the puck, and guess what? It lands right smack on Jordan's stick. There are now five seconds remaining in a deadlocked state championship final game, and Jordan has the puck and nobody between him and the opposing goalie. He sprints for the net, shoots for the top corner, and scores!

. . .

As this story demonstrates, no matter what the challenge, you never know how things will ultimately turn out. Most of the time, the final work of art takes on an entirely different shape than the artist originally planned. One secret to success and contentment is to take stock in the quality of your thoughts and feelings in the moment, and allow your mind to self-correct (the murky water to clear). Then—with clarity and awareness at your side—insights will flow and answers will become obvious. When the penalty was called on Jordan, wayward thinking abounded. The coach, the fans, and even Jordan, at first, perceived the circumstances as disastrous. After all, who could blame them? This was the state finals. However, while the initial thought of disappointment is quite normal, Jordan looked within—to a place deeper than those reactionary thoughts—and discovered that the chance for creating something better always existed.

The True Path to Learning from a Loss

But what if things hadn't turned out so well for Jordan? What if he failed to permit his murky thoughts to quiet? What if, instead of being in the right spot at the right time, the game simply ended and his team lost? Indeed, when athletes fail, I am often asked to define the "appropriate response." Should a player be so disturbed that he or she is inconsolable? How about knocking over a water cooler? How about laughing off the disappointment? How about not shaking hands with the victorious team?

The answer, you might be surprised, is that I will never define how a player or a coach should behave in defeat, victory, or any other situation. An individual's conduct is completely personal, and in no way will I hinder a player's or coach's free will by putting boundaries on what he or she is *supposed* to do.

I will, on the other hand, turn my attention toward the level of well-being of the particular player or coach during each situation. Which brings us to the recurrent theme of this book: When an individual is able to recognize the thinking and internal feelings that accompany a clear and assured level of psychological functioning, and commit to acting *only* from this state, then the proper behavior will naturally follow. Let's use one of today's most well-known athletes as an example.

After the last game of the 2009 NBA Eastern Conference Finals, LeBron James, who then played for the team that lost the series, the Cleveland Cavaliers, decided not to shake hands with players from the victorious Orlando

Magic. Many outsiders believed that James, being one of the premier and most popular stars in the league, had set an example of poor sportsmanship and that he should apologize. James, however, remained resolute in his actions. Even though he was extremely disappointed with the loss, he insisted his thinking was clear at that moment—he simply didn't feel that the time was right to offer congratulations to the opposing players. To those who were quick to judge, I would note that no league or team rules were violated. Perhaps James even averted a volatile situation by immediately choosing to head to the locker room to regroup with his teammates. We just don't know.

But let's go back to the initial question of what to teach players in the face of a challenging predicament or tough loss. The real trick to growing from this type of negative (or even positive) experience, I believe, is to allow your own thinking and gut feelings to be your guide, not to behave in a certain prescribed manner. Once again, I will never define an action, such as knocking over a water cooler or refusing to shake hands, as right or wrong. What I will do is remind players and coaches that, regardless of the events of the outside world, prolific choices are made from clear mental functioning, fluent thinking, and affirmative feelings.

Clear Thinking: Essential for Success On and Off the Field

When working with athletes, I obviously focus much of my attention on the principle of thought. So I am often asked if individuals can use their thinking to enhance their athletic experience and be more successful. Well, as I said, you can't manage your thoughts, but you can utilize your understanding of the principle of thought for this purpose.

Here's an illustration: Baseball pitchers at the high school or even collegiate level step onto a different type of pitching mound at every game. Some mounds are high; some are low; some are soft; some are firm; some have a deep hole at the rubber; some have hardly any hole at all. When a pitcher takes the field at the beginning of a game, he has the ability to allow his thinking to make whatever type of mound he encounters into his favorite type. If there is a deep hole, he might say, "Great, I can create more push off." If there is hardly any hole, he might say, "Great, I can create more leverage." You get the picture.

Another way to consider it is: If you are an athlete or coach, it is crucial that you look inward to the value of your thoughts, feelings, and moods throughout the course of any competition. Are they low and unproductive? Or are they fluent and empowering? Once this question is answered—and you recognize the nature of your own thinking—you will then see (like our young hockey player Jordan) that it is possible to think and thus believe that any situation is there to help you.

One more thing: Rest assured that even the most consistent athletes in the world, at times, think negative thoughts. The "clutch" player, however, possesses a secret that the average guys haven't tapped into. Although he might not be able to explain it, this type of player realizes that his current state of mind is the creator of his negative thoughts; these thoughts are not real. As soon as his mind-set changes, the player's view of life and his thoughts will change, too. This understanding—*not* trying to do something about errant thoughts—allows the minds of the most resilient achievers to quiet down in the midst of negativity. Such stillpower permits positive feelings and the potential for success to emerge spontaneously.

5

THE ULTIMATE COACHING DILEMMA: AN ATHLETE'S STATE OF MIND VERSUS BEHAVIOR

*The fool only knows what he thinks;
the wise man knows he's the thinker.*
SYDNEY BANKS

Michael is an outstanding young baseball player, but he is late for a meeting with Coach Kline, his high school baseball coach and a man who requires his players to be punctual. Seventeen years of age and a new driver, Michael gets lost on the way to the coach's office. He calls Coach Kline in a panic and says, "Coach, I am totally lost. I have no idea where I am. I took a wrong turn, and now I'm in the middle of nowhere. I'm getting really frustrated."

Coach Kline tells Michael to calm down, but just as he does, the phone goes dead. He tries to call back but to no avail. About an hour later, an upset Coach Kline looks out his window and sees Michael's car pulling into the parking lot. Thankfully, his player has found his way. Yet, as Michael gets closer and closer, Coach Kline can see that the front end of the car is smashed. Michael's been in an accident.

Now Coach Kline is really perturbed. He springs from his chair; he's going to give his tardy player a piece of his mind. The words are already forming in the coach's head: *Focus when you're driving, Michael; no cell phone; keep the proper distance between your car and the car in front of you.* If this happens again, Michael could get hurt and might be lost for the season. Coach Kline is considering teaching Michael a lesson about responsibility by handing down a one-game suspension!

As he arrives outside, however, Coach Kline sees that Michael is extremely shaken. As a result, Coach Kline's thinking alters in an instant, and a sense of compassion floods through him. He hugs his star player, and they walk arm in arm into the office. When they sit down, Coach Kline realizes something profound: Michael is a responsible young man, he knows that he should be focused when driving, and he certainly understands what the proper distance is between cars. So what caused the crash in the first place?

Like a thunderbolt, it insightfully hits Coach Kline that the accident was the direct result of Michael's confused state of mind in the moment; it had nothing to do with his behavior. From an aggravated level of psychological functioning, born from his thoughts about getting lost and being late, Michael's consciousness descended and the perceptual field closed up on him. He simply could not judge the proper distance, and when the car in front of him stopped, bang! It was as simple as that.

. . .

The lesson to be learned here is obviously not about focus, speaking on the phone while driving, or behavior in any form. Like other examples in this book, it is about recognizing where our well-being, state of mind, or consciousness rests in the moment—and being guided from that viewpoint. Luckily, Coach Kline grasped this understanding and immediately switched gears. Rather than punish Michael, he lovingly reminded him to be on guard when his mood is low and his thoughts are racing—because that's when his actions will be most troublesome. What would have happened if Coach Kline had judged Michael's behavior and disciplined him? No doubt Michael would have broken down or stormed out, and the outstanding teaching opportunity would have been lost forever.

Here is another departure from current thinking, this time pertaining to the principle of consciousness: Since it is never productive to make assumptions or judgments about the reasons for someone else's actions, if you are a coach, look to the state of mind of your players instead. A coaching methodology that focuses on behaviors is solely mentoring in the past.

Far too many coaches (teachers, parents, and employers as well) take the state of mind of their team for granted and then wonder why the best-laid plans don't work. In other words, if the team's collective level of consciousness is low, even well-thought-out strategies will be ineffective. If consciousness is high, you just might beat the New York Yankees. Either way, if you can impart this understanding and lesson as Coach Kline did, you will have found the hidden truth behind effective sports psychology and enduring player-coach relationships.

Why Focusing on Behavior Guarantees Fallout

Coaches who fail to tap into their players' level of consciousness run the risk of unintentionally contributing to, among other things, a severe decrease in performance—

especially if the player also fails to understand this important principle. This notion brings us back to the concept of team rules. As introduced in chapter 3, I clearly recognize that coaches must set specific guidelines for their teams. Rules and expectations, though, should only be instituted (or amended) by a coach when he or she is operating from a fluent state of mind, *never* in the heat of the moment.

As an example, let's look at an episode involving talented Miami Marlins third baseman Hanley Ramirez, a player with virtually no history of behavioral issues. In the second inning of a 2010 game versus the Arizona Diamondbacks, Ramirez committed a costly error and then, after accidentally kicking the ball, loafed after it, allowing two runners to score. He was then benched the next inning by manager Fredi González.[1] What followed were several days of negative press for Ramirez for his lack of effort, a war of words between player and coach, a forced apology from Ramirez, and soon after, the dismissal of González as the Marlins' manager. I obviously don't know all the internal details, but it seems to me that the benching of a player should never lead to such bitterness or unfortunate consequences.

To be forthright, González should not, I believe, have excused Ramirez's lack of effort. If he was thinking clearly and felt the benching was warranted, that is definitely his prerogative as manager. However, in order for the situation to have ended that night, and for González to have actually helped Ramirez (and his team), it was essential that González look past his player's behavior to its source. For a professional athlete to loaf, he must be operating from a low level of well-being. So, because no one is open to advice when his well-being is low, González's reaction—his harsh private and public criticism—only exacerbated Ramirez's low level of functioning. Again, benching a player for lack of effort was not the real issue for Fredi González. Not understanding the cause behind the lack of effort, and thus not giving the player the time and space for his state of mind to clear, was.

When an athlete (or any of us) exists in a low state of mind, it is impossible to perform at an elevated level. One's effort will only be as high as one's level of consciousness at that particular moment. An angry player can only play angry. A frustrated player can only play frustrated. A despondent player can only play despondently. The correlation is direct and immediate. And if a coach or player lacks this understanding (and continues to look outside for causes and solutions), the results will almost always be regrettable.

About now, you might be asking yourself, "I'm starting to recognize the importance in looking toward the principle of consciousness, but exactly how am I supposed to use it to enhance my performance?" Or, "What should any coach, teacher, or parent do when a challenging predicament (like the Ramirez/González situation) occurs?"

My answer will not surprise you. First, it is imperative that you maintain your own level of psychological balance. Second, recognize that when mentoring or disciplining, the behavior of the individual in question is relatively insignificant. If consciousness descends, effort and performance (behavior) will most probably follow. Third, do not impart advice at this time—the individual is not seeing life clearly so he or she is not capable of perceiving the value in advice. Instead, do whatever feels right to you, from a loving perspective, to help the individual raise his or her level of well-being. This, I should add, is where Fredi González stumbled in his dealings with Hanley Ramirez.

Finally, back to the basic understanding to which we should all hold ourselves accountable: Teach your players, students, or children that "challenging" external circumstances have zero ability to regulate their lives in any way. While it may look like your revved-up thoughts are the result of a particular situation, these thoughts are actually the result of your current level of consciousness. If your thoughts are flowing and you're feeling secure, move forward. If your thoughts are stuck and you're feeling anxious, be still.

The Principle of Consciousness and Tiger Woods

This liberating message certainly applies to life outside of the athletic arena as well. Sometimes my work revolves around not only performance issues but helping athletes who find themselves in personal predicaments much like what Tiger Woods experienced in 2009, when his extramarital affairs were revealed.

All of us, even the world's best athletes, succeed or fail based on our current state of mind or level of consciousness. Everything we do—all of our decisions, in fact—are at the mercy of this critical mental factor. Decisions made from higher states of mind are more likely to work out well. Decisions made from lower, less aware states of mind are more likely to be misguided or challenging. To illustrate this paradigm, let's look closely at the plight of Tiger Woods.

When Tiger was young, his father constantly reminded him about the out-of-bounds stakes and water hazards that existed on all golf courses.[2] As opposed to most sports psychologists or golf coaches who would instruct their players not to think about these hazards, Earl Woods knew that, from time to time, during a tournament, a thought about these danger spots was bound to pop into his son's head. As a result, Tiger learned not to be duped by his own thoughts. Major championships followed.

Tiger failed, however, to apply the same understanding to his life away from the game of golf. He overlooked one of the most significant messages of this book: A person's state of mind will always determine one's ability to regulate urges. When one's state of mind is high, a wayward thought does not inspire wayward action. When one's state of mind is low, a person is not capable of seeing life clearly, so he or she is prone to serious lapses in judgment and acting on impulses. Remember, our state of mind, our consciousness, is the source of our view on life—not the effect. Until a person accepts this principle, he or she is vulnerable to whatever his or her mind creates at that particular moment and likely to repeat the same mistakes.

This is both an overlooked and crucial aspect of the human experience. Just reflect on your own most memorable mistakes. Were your faulty judgments, and resulting poor behavior, about the situation you were in—or about your state of mind at the moment you encountered the situation? I often instruct my clients that when they are in a low state of mind, they must completely distrust their thoughts and ensuing feelings. For if they act on these misleading thoughts, they will slip up, on or off the field (or golf course), 100 percent of the time.

The Ultimate Explanation for Any Type of Behavior

About a year ago, I was asked to give a talk to a group of parents on another behavioral issue: the acute subject of bullying in youth sports today. How I approached this often-discussed topic surprised the audience and will help further clarify the basic premise of this chapter.

As I explained to the parents that day, the issue at hand is not the behavior of bullying; the issue is the state of mind that leads to the behavior of bullying. It seems paradoxical, but the behavior, bullying, is only the after-effect. This perspective is difficult for many people to grasp. They react to what they see. If the behavior or act doesn't look right or meet with their approval, they think it needs to be fixed. However, fixing behavior (for bullies, the standard course of action would be teaching respect and sensitivity) does not get to its root cause. Respect and sensitivity are the result of one thing: a high level of consciousness. And the young person who bullies is making decisions when his or her level of consciousness is extremely low. If he or she were in a high state of mind, bullying would not occur.

To help eliminate bullying, then, it was necessary for these parents to first appreciate, and then hold their children accountable to, a message often applied in this book: A person's thoughts and feelings will always be the perfect indicators of his or her current state of mind. Negative thoughts and feelings are not a sign to proceed (bully) but rather a call to do nothing until the low mind-set passes, clarity sets in, and the same circumstances are viewed differently.

During the presentation, I also addressed the state of mind of the person being bullied. The same understanding applies. Parents, coaches, and teachers need a delicate touch to teach a young person that it is actually *possible* to feel compassion for a bully, but *impossible* for the actions of another person to reduce one's level of contentment or self-worth. This brings us back to the importance of looking inward to your own thoughts and feelings moment to moment. If you are thinking clearly and you walk away from a bully, fine. If you are thinking clearly and decide to confront the bully, then that too is fine. Being the victim of a bully is never contingent on the bully. It is a harsh reality that only occurs when your level of consciousness is low; when this level is high, a bully's antics are much more manageable.

Here is a departure from conventional thinking that may be difficult for some of us to accept. Our perceptions are always subject to change, so that means that our problems *must* be generated from inside of us—and not coming from the world out there. The subject of bullying perfectly exemplifies this attitude. Only when a bully begins to understand *why* he acts in the first place (his state of mind is low), and the bullied individual begins to see *why* these actions affect him negatively (same reason), will we find the answer to the conduct on both sides. As I reminded the audience that day, the first step is to look away from the outward behavior in question and inward toward a person's state of mind, or level of consciousness, at that particular point in time.

Performance, State of Mind, and the UConn Women

Let's discuss the overwhelming success of the University of Connecticut women's basketball team as a final example of the power of the principle of consciousness. Like many sports fans across the country, I am in awe of the record-setting UConn winning streak (which ended at ninety games on December 30, 2010) as well as the back-to-back national titles and the constant stream of All-Americans produced by this program.

To put this achievement in perspective, winning ninety straight games is the equivalent of going unde-feated through an entire pro basketball or hockey season, plus two playoff rounds. It is comparable to going five and a half years without a loss in the NFL. While I personally don't believe the national press has ever given this team and coach their due, following the 2010 Women's Final Four, I did hear some sportscasters talk with admiration about the team's focus, poise, work ethic, and intensity.

I, too, believe the above traits have been key ingredi-ents in UConn's enduring success. Yet there exists an underlying factor at work here that no one seemed to recognize at the time, let alone ever talked about. As we are now aware, to maintain such an elevated level of consistency, an individual or team must first be operating from an elevated level of well-being or consciousness. Understanding the principle of consciousness is the num-ber one attribute necessary to ensure steady play and unwavering success. Focus, poise, work ethic, and intensity have to come from somewhere, and I am certain that this principle is the first place to look.

As proof, let's turn our attention to what happened in the Women's National Championship game in 2010. In the opening half versus Stanford, UConn simply couldn't get out of its own way offensively. Players couldn't make a shot, couldn't find lanes to the hoop, and almost collided with each other about a dozen times. They did, however, maintain their defensive vision and strategy. Hence, they scored an all-time low twelve points, but only gave up twenty. At intermission, victory was still within reach.

To the reporters who interviewed UConn coach Geno Auriemma right then, however, there appeared to be a problem. When asked what he said to his players in the locker room after such an unexpected (and disastrous) first half, Auriemma replied, "I didn't have anything to say, so I said nothing except to slow things down." The reporters were shocked. Where was the motivational pep talk? What about a new offensive strategy?

These reporters undoubtedly fell into the common trap of believing that in order to succeed, a coach must address the behavior or performance of his players. This is not necessarily the case. At this stage of the game, Coach Auriemma's silence was amazingly astute and, as a result, I am certain he averted a host of issues that would have led his team to an unanticipated loss.

How did he accomplish this feat? Although he might not be able to describe it, Auriemma grasps the principle of consciousness. That night he refused to try to fix the "off" performance by altering the external situation at hand. He realized that his (and his players') level of psychological functioning had dropped so, at that moment, he was incapable of finding a solution to the dreadful first half. In short, Auriemma trusted it was only a matter of time before he and his talented team regained awareness and got back on track—he simply allowed his players to manifest the victory within reach.

That's the way the best teams and coaches usually operate: They know that the game (and life) is always the best teacher, and if we allow our minds to be still, consciousness will rise and the answers, including the strategy for attacking the basket, will eventually come. It sounds ridiculously simple but, again, the most insightful coaches and players never forget that remarkable performance is always right around the corner. And if it doesn't show up that night—well, the opportunity exists to create something worthwhile out of that, too.

6

THE NEUTRALITY OF THE OUTSIDE WORLD

You can always improve your life situation,
but you can never improve your life.
ECKHART TOLLE

At the outset of just about every talk I give, I ask the audience for their thoughts on what makes certain athletes clutch. Audience members usually throw out a variety of attributes, such as composure, toughness, hard work, fortitude, and confidence. While rarely is an answer off the mark, I would argue that the true source of coming through in the big moments revolves around an athlete's understanding and application of his or her own free will. The empowering belief that you are free to get out on the playing field and just let go provides all the answers to performing under pressure that you will ever need.

Clutch athletes, the Los Angeles Lakers' Kobe Bryant being a perfect example, feel practically no restrictions when they are playing their sport. They play with freedom. The surprising reason that Bryant makes so many important shots on the basketball court: he knows that he will be perfectly okay—even if he misses. It may appear that basketball is life and death to Bryant but, believe me, there is no way all those miracle shots would happen if he gave in to this type of desperate thinking.

Life, Life Situations, and Freedom

One way to help crystallize this paradigm is to recognize the inherent difference between your life and the life situations that you encounter every day. Life situations are: the pitch you are about to throw, the shot you are about to take, where you are chosen in the NFL draft, asking someone out for a date. Although it might not seem so at this moment, the outcome of any life situation, regardless of how it may be perceived, is purely neutral.

We don't, however, tend to think of life events or situations in terms of neutrality. We usually judge and/or assign them a value: positive or negative, good or bad, helpful or hurtful. If you throw a strike, for instance, you're up; if you get turned down for a date, you're down.

Yet, regardless of how you feel about the situations you face, your life is a constant. While most of us think that external circumstances actually happen to us, in truth they don't. They're just happening. All life situations are just happening. Granted, we play a role in the outcome of whatever it is we face, but regardless of our role or whether we're happy or disappointed, the nature of all circumstances or results in life is unbiased. This basic understanding is essential in your quest for success.

As a case in point, let's consider the career path of another clutch athlete: Tom Brady of the New England Patriots. Did you know (before he won three Super Bowl titles) that he was not selected until the sixth round of the 2000 NFL draft out of Michigan? Was he, in the moment, happy about it? Probably not. Did he understand that his draft status possessed zero ability to regulate his life and thus his future success or failure? My guess is absolutely yes.

Simply put, Brady recognized the neutrality of his life situation. But the ability to distinguish between life and life situations does not always come without difficulty. Recently, I met with a successful NHL player who was particularly headstrong about this concept. He was struggling to score goals and in a low mood that he just couldn't shake. After we spoke for a while, I told him that it was time to understand that hockey was his passion, his profession, and he loved the game, but it was not his life. He wasn't buying it (since he had been told many times that the opposite was true); in fact, he almost walked out of my office. That's when I decided to use a rather drastic illustration. I said, "Let's suppose I placed ten pucks at center ice and asked you to shoot the first nine into an open net at one end of the rink. How many would you make?"

He responded without hesitation, "All nine."

I then said (and I apologize for this gruesome analogy), "On the last puck, I'm going to walk out to center ice and put a pistol to your head. If you miss, I'm going to pull the trigger. What would happen on that shot?"

At first he offered that he would still make it. Then, the more he thought, the more he began to waffle. Until, in the end, he flat out admitted that he would probably miss the tenth shot.

What does this illustration show? Performing any task or activity while believing the outcome will somehow be indicative of your self-worth (not neutral), or believing the activity can somehow regulate your life (a gun to your head), is a surefire way to lower your consciousness and shrink the perceptual field. My client, the hockey player, was sitting comfortably in my office just thinking about the possible scenario, and things started to close up for him.

The lesson, and its potentially freeing feeling, is this: Sometimes it will look like external events do, in reality, possess the power to determine your level of contentment or success. But this is simply because your emotions, such as elation when you win or dejection when you lose, are temporarily diverting your attention away from your current thoughts and mood. Only when you understand that your level of contentment is not regulated by external desires—the number of goals you score, birdies you make, strikes you throw, or even the amount of money you have in the bank—will the odds dramatically increase that you will create more of what you desire.

More precisely, if you can sense the difference between what goes on in the outside world (life situations) and the resolute nature of your inner world (your life), you will be one of the fortunate few to uncover the true source of our innate freedom. It is this freedom that allows you to make everything that occurs productive. It is this freedom that makes anything possible.

Goals, Rewards, and the Journey

To take this paradigm a step further, let's consider the common prerequisite for almost every athlete or coach at the beginning of a game, a season, or even a career: goal setting. The neutrality of life events is the primary reason that I am not a big fan of this practice. Quite simply (and I realize that this sounds a little corny), I prefer dreams over goals. When we dream of a certain result, insights always flow. We tend not to get weighed down by whether it happens or not. When we set goals, we have a hard time separating ourselves from outcomes. If we don't reach our goal, we often think there must be something wrong with us. To put it bluntly, too many people today (including athletes) believe that a set goal represents the source of their happiness.

To the contrary, when we see the potential in embracing the process or journey, rewards become bountiful. The reward may be our initial dream but, more often than not, the vision ultimately takes on a new reality. For example, if you asked most contented and successful individuals who love their work how they ended up in their current occupation, I bet 99 percent would respond, "Come to think about it, I have no idea." They started out on their career journey, and the twists and turns of life somehow created the appropriate destination.

What's really interesting is that most people immersed in this type of creative-based journey rarely perform an action because they feel they *must* do it. They act because they *want* to. They don't renegotiate their contract, reach out to their coach, or go to the gym because they need to—they do it because it feels right. So they rarely stumble.

In the revealing book *Drive*, motivation expert and author Daniel H. Pink describes the above pattern in terms of how schools and corporations reward success.[1] He actually found that both students and workers become more imaginative and efficient at performing a task if there isn't a reward or goal on the other end. Just think about that. We perform better when we get caught up in the experience, rather than when we make the experience about us. Reason being—unlike the strategy of most coaches today—when we focus on a personal prize, our options narrow; when we relish the process, our options expand. As we discussed, the power to create lies within us, not in the outside world's reward-based judgment of what we accomplish.

This perspective, I should add, is not to suggest that the practice of goal setting is good, bad, or indifferent. If your goal is to win, that is certainly worthwhile. Who doesn't want to win? But because winning has no ability to regulate your happiness or what you should ever think about yourself, using goals as a life barometer will always be a self-defeating prophecy. Granted, if you are truly relishing life's journey and experiences, and a goal (or better yet, a dream) still appears to be necessary, then it is perfectly fine to go for it. My suggestion, however, is to remain open to the neutrality of each step along the way and to where the creative quest might ultimately take you.

Routine and Potential

In contrast to this viewpoint of staying open to the fluidity and creativity of life and, in turn, increasing the odds for success, the world of athletics is currently rife with coaches, commentators, and sports psychologists preaching to players about the need to develop dependable and unwavering habits or routines. It is commonly believed that routines are necessary for consistently positive behavior, and it is often said that sticking to a routine will help you to come through in a clutch moment. While some routines are valuable—the routine of kissing your spouse or children goodnight, for example—I think it is important to look closely at routines and their potentially unconstructive effects.

A routine is okay until it becomes more significant than the task at hand. Or, put another way, until it prevents you from following your gut instinct. In the world of sports, routines that do not change, evolve, or grow with the athlete, coach, or parent will always hamper imagination and performance. While listening to a sports radio program in New York, I once heard commentators debating why New York Jets coach Rex Ryan (whose team started the season 2–0) chose to accept the ball upon winning the coin flip at the start of the Jets' third game in 2009. In the first two weeks of the season, Ryan had won the toss and chosen to start the game with his defensive team each time. The commentators were baffled. Why would Ryan deviate from the routine that was so successful in the first two games?

That Ryan might have insightfully strategized that starting out on offense was best, at that moment, never even crossed their minds. And while I can't exactly say what Ryan was thinking, if his instincts were telling him to take the ball, but his routine said to kick, then my advice would be to grab the ball 100 percent of the time.

So, do the routines of professional athletes or coaches actually help or hinder performance? What do we potentially sacrifice by relying on routines? Let's dig deeper into the sport of golf to find the answers. These days, behavioral coaches, swing coaches, and golf broadcasters often insist that you must go through the same routine before every shot you hit. From the first swing of the day to the last, if you are consistent with your preshot routine, you will be a more consistent player, according to the experts.

What then is a player supposed to do when the routine isn't working and he or she is playing inconsistently? Or, what if the routine doesn't feel right that day or on a particular shot, will the player actually be successful if he or she goes through with it anyway? Of course not. But more importantly, I believe that in stressing routines, many coaches are creating robotic and somewhat obsessive athletes who are failing to learn to use the power of their own insights to overcome a challenge.

Just think for a minute about the most successful and dynamic people in any walk of life; they are always the ones who have creatively stepped outside the box to find the answers. From artists like the Beatles to coaches like Herb Brooks, these individuals knew that drawing up a game plan was essential; yet more significantly, they were wise enough to go with their instinct when it told them to alter the strategy.

The Beatles' original drummer was a childhood friend of John Lennon and Paul McCartney named Pete Best. Although the group's managers were comfortable sticking to a routine that was starting to take hold, Lennon and McCartney had the gut feeling that a wackier and more flamboyant partner on the drums would serve them better. Consequently, the legend of Ringo Starr was born.

By 1980 Herb Brooks had run a successful national-championship-winning system as the hockey coach at the University of Minnesota. It was, therefore, expected that he would simply bring this system along as he took the reins of the US Olympic hockey team. Brooks, however, reflected that his standard strategy and old training routines would have little impact against the quicker moving international competition. So he boldly broke away from his comfortable coaching routine, and the rest is well-known sports lore.

What these examples show is that creativity, vision, and free will are absolutely essential for you to separate yourself from what everybody else in your sport (or in life) is doing. In sticking to the same old routines—before making a golf swing, in a management decision, or in our daily lives—we eventually get tired and stale. We then begin to question our lack of motivation and enjoyment, and revved-up thoughts cloud the task at hand. Ultimately, we buy into the judgments of the outside world and settle for second best.

As a freeing alternative, why not trust your own inner voice when you hear it call? In going with their gut instinct, and understanding it, the Beatles and Coach

Brooks built brilliant consistency, not routine consistency. They knew that true success would only originate from pure insight—not from stale ideas and never from playing it safe.

Leaving School with Wisdom

All too often, we forget to listen to our powerful and insightful gut feelings. We forget that external neutral circumstances have no regulatory power over us—these life situations cannot create the contentment that we crave.

To illustrate this understanding, let's talk about the difficult decision that confronts numerous exceptional young athletes as they choose between finishing their schooling or going directly to the pros. Every year as the NBA draft nears, sports radio fires up a discussion about the rule that a player must be either nineteen years of age or one year removed from the graduation of his high school class to be eligible for the NBA draft. The debate centers on money. As commentator Mike Golic argued on ESPN's *Mike and Mike in the Morning*, "There is life-changing money out there. Shouldn't these young players be allowed to grab it while they are physi-cally able to do so?"

Now I'm not going to debate the NBA rule, but I do want to comment on the emphasis placed on "life-changing money." Money, fame, or adulation are just more examples of external situations that have no ability to alter a person's life, and broadcasting this flawed viewpoint only serves to distort this crucial understanding. Yes, money can satisfy external wants such as a house, a car, or even a trust fund for your family. But life and the potential for contentment and success, regardless of one's current circumstances, are steadfast for everyone. And until this lesson is clearly imparted and understood by commentators and coaches, I believe the question of the appropriate age to enter the NBA is moot.

The same goes for the entry programs, which were created by professional sports leagues (specifically the NBA and the NFL), to counteract the unruly choices commonly made by rookies. Leagues have hired behavioral experts and security details to guide young players as they embark upon their professional journeys. On the surface these types of policies sound sensible, and I applaud the front offices of the NBA and the NFL for considering the welfare of their players. The problem, though, is that the leagues are actually contributing to the insecure thinking of the same individuals whom they are trying to protect. And here's why:

These programs demonstrate that the surrounding circumstances, or temptations, of professional sports have the power to regulate one's thinking, choices, or life. When, as we know, this is not possible. Again, why teach young athletes that they must manage behavior and encourage them to become passive victims of their own careers and lives? Why not provide the understanding that they need not be controlled by external circumstances in the first place?

These questions bring us directly back to the one we started with: When is the appropriate time to leave school for the bright lights of big-league sports? The time is only right, I think, when a player deeply understands that one's life situation has no ability to regulate one's life. This intuitive concept, looking inside of oneself for answers (including when to ask for help), is what the talk-show hosts should be broadcasting and the NBA and the NFL should be teaching. Once he looks within, a young athlete will always see that the opportunity exists to create the proper path from the current situation, no matter how good or bad it might appear. Dictating to impressionable young minds about how to behave or when to leave school only exacerbates the quandary by fostering a dependence on outer resources.

7
SPORTS, JUDGMENT, AND LIFE FROM THE INSIDE OUT

*We don't see things as they are;
we see them as we are.*
Anaïs Nin

Roberto De Vicenzo, the renowned Argentinian professional golfer, once won a tournament with a substantial cash prize. After receiving his check and smiling through interviews and photos, he went to the clubhouse and prepared to leave. Sometime later, as he walked to his car in the parking lot, he was approached by a young woman. She offered well wishes on the victory and then told him that her baby was seriously ill and near death, but she had no money to pay the doctors' bills and hospital expenses. De Vicenzo was so moved by her story that right on the spot, he took out a pen and endorsed the winning check over to the woman.

"Make some good days for the child," he said as he pressed the check into her hand.

The following week, De Vicenzo was having lunch at the next tour stop when a PGA official approached him. "Several members of the parking lot crew told me you met a young woman after the tournament last week," he said.

De Vicenzo nodded. "Well," said the official, "I hate to tell you—she's a phony. She has no sick kid. I'm sorry, my friend, but that girl fleeced you."

De Vicenzo responded, "You mean there's no dying baby?"

"That's right."

"That's the best news I've heard all week," De Vicenzo answered.[1]

· · ·

I was first introduced to this poignant story and its message many years ago by Alan Cohen. To me, it exemplifies the understanding that external circumstances have no power to regulate one's thinking, feelings, decisions, or life. Ultimately, we have no ability to control the actions of others, but we all possess the potential to understand that these actions have no ability to control us. While some may classify De Vicenzo's generous act as ignorant or even foolish, he knew the winner's purse was far more essential to a distressed mother than it was to him. And then, discovering there was one less sick child in the world was more important to De Vicenzo than allowing his thoughts about a desperate scam to get the better of him.

The lesson here is simple: When we act from clarity, it is impossible to get weighed down by judgmental outcomes. Just reflect for a moment: When your choices originate from high levels of well-being and positive feelings, do you care what other people think? Do you care what they do with these choices?

De Vicenzo won an immense total of 230 golf tournaments worldwide in his career. More remarkably, however, he used this notoriety to bring relief and hope to millions of people in his homeland of Argentina. As this story illustrates, when we live life from the inside out, it becomes extremely easy to act in harmony with our own values, swim with the flow of life, and triumph. De Vicenzo knew that he, not external events, was in charge. This understanding made him both a compassionate human being and an awesome competitor.

The Understanding of an Icon

I often broach the following subject during my presentations or seminars: Athletes and coaches who adopt a universal perspective—who make their journey about something greater than their own accomplishments—will perform freely and will consistently create success. They will also, I am certain, have a greater impact on their teammates, families, and communities. When a person reaches this height of consciousness, he or she is compassionate and competitive. The perceptual field expands, both on the field and in everyday life.

Roberto De Vicenzo possessed this inside-out understanding, as did other extraordinary athletes throughout history. One such individual was Jackie Robinson. Robinson is remembered for being the man who broke the color barrier in Major League Baseball. A Hall of Famer, his number, 42, hangs in every park in the big leagues. Although most admirers recall the fortitude and courage that propelled Robinson to greatness in the face of extreme prejudice and believe it was the bigotry that fueled his passion, I would like to provide a different viewpoint on the success of this beloved American hero.

Jackie Robinson, like De Vicenzo, was completely aware that his existence was untouchable by any external circumstance. He knew that nothing or no one could stand between him and the game of baseball—and more notably, the game of life. Racial slurs, objects hurled from the stands, and hatred ingrained by generations of prejudice had no ability to slow him down. Robinson's state of mind was so secure that he declined to judge these peripheral (and neutral) situations—thus he never deterred himself from pursuing his passions. His secret, I believe, was the pure understanding that personal freedom and one's perception of life are 100 percent self-determined.

This secret, or understanding, does not imply that Robinson was okay with prejudice, not at all. In fact, he dedicated much of his life away from the game of baseball to the civil rights movement. He once said, "There's not an American in this country free until every one of us is free."[2] However, by remaining aware of his innate potential to perceive life from the inside out (not vice versa), Robinson stayed open to the inherent goodness and productive possibilities in all situations and people. This is why, regardless of external factors, he contributed with vision beyond his time to the eradication of the thinking behind narrow-minded hate.

While teammate Duke Snider was most likely referring to Robinson's on-field exploits when calling him the "greatest competitor I have ever seen,"[3] I would argue that Robinson's real competitiveness evolved from the fundamental understanding that our judgments exist as a result of our own thinking, independent of the world around us. This understanding kept Robinson at a higher plane of consciousness than most others—one step ahead. And it provided all the answers, both on and off the field, to any apparent challenge that came his way.

• • •

Hereafter, whenever you allow the external circumstances in life to get you down, I suggest you consider the life of Jackie Robinson, the choices of Roberto De Vicenzo, and the examples of resilience and understanding that they set. Both of these outstanding athletes recognized that there was never a reason, no matter how bleak things appeared on the outside, not to hope for the possibility of something better. In turn, they used the natural gifts, which exist at everyone's inner disposal, to make an enduring difference for themselves and their fellow man. As Jackie Robinson once said, "Life is not a spectator sport. If you're going to spend your whole life in the grandstand just watching what goes on, you're simply wasting your life."[4]

The Resilience to Move Forward

All too often, popular culture, not to mention popular psychology, attributes our attainments or resilience to judgments about elements outside of ourselves. An emotional article, "Pursuit of Gold Medal Moves Burke Forward," written by Yahoo! Sports columnist Dan Wetzel on February 16, 2010, provides an example of this flawed perspective.

In this article, Wetzel talks about the US Olympic Men's Ice Hockey Team's general manager, Brian Burke, and how he "coped" with the tragic death of his youngest son, Brendan, just prior to the opening of the 2010 Winter Olympic Games. Wetzel astutely alludes to Burke's valor, determination, and desire to provide the proper leadership for both his family and his team. He mentions that at that moment, and in spite of his misfortune, Burke was hard at work spearheading the efforts of his young American players and coaching staff. There is one serious error in this story, however—the title.

It is not possible for the pursuit of a gold medal to move Brian Burke forward. Only a deep understanding of how human beings shape their experiences, paired with a resilient faith, can do this. I maintain that articles and opinions like Wetzel's are making the innocent but destructive mistake of confusing inner fortitude and wisdom with outer goals, diversions, and judgments.

Don't get me wrong, I am well versed in the positives of immersing oneself thoroughly in a project. But this type of placebo will never help Burke to put (as Wetzel said in the article) "one foot in front of the other" and carry on. The ability to persevere comes from within; in no way should it be tied to the fate of an external factor such as an eager group of young athletes.

So then, how does the above understanding serve individuals and families when this type of calamity strikes? It may not be obvious at first, but, as we have seen in this book, everything that takes place "out there"—every failure, every mistake, every loss—occurs to clarify our path, not to obscure it. When faced with what looks like an unscalable tragedy, our calling is to look inward and allow ourselves to find its true source and meaning. Rather than sequestering our emotions through external escapes, the opportunity always exists to create purpose through any heartbreak, no matter how challenging it might appear. It is this understanding that carried Burke through—not altering his focus and "plowing into evaluating hockey teams," as Wetzel put it.

Brian Burke found his own inner strength by offering compassionate support to his family and his team in the midst of tragedy. His example truly shows that when life is lived from the inside out, it becomes possible to make sense of any situation, even the most heart-wrenching of circumstances such as a loved one's death.

The Fallacy of Bulletin-Board Material

Here is another fallacy about the power of external diversion. Throughout my growth as a young hockey player, like many athletes, I was often subjected to unwritten rules that were supposed to make a player or team more successful—if only faith was placed in such external "truths." For example, I had many coaches who cautioned us about speaking disparagingly, especially in public, about our opponents. The common thought system was then, and still is today, that you don't want to provide the other team with fodder for "bulletin-board material." Reason being you might give the opposition added incentive to hate you, and thus more motivation to want to kick your butt on the field, court, or ice.

Like virtually all athletes, the notion sounded right to me so, I bought in. As I moved on to play high school and college hockey, I refused to even mention my opponents during press interviews for fear of potentially saying the wrong thing. Then one day during my junior year at Hamilton, several days before our yearly matchup with Colgate University, one of Colgate's players commented in the local paper that "puny" Hamilton didn't belong on the same ice with the more seasoned Colgate squad.

Well, you guessed it. The day before the big game, the article was posted on the bulletin board in our locker room. And man, did it tick us off! Just as my former coaches had indicated, my teammates and I wanted to rip the heads off the rival players from Colgate. For the rest of the day, through our practice and during our pregame meal, all we could think about was getting out there and sticking it to those guys. Finally, it was game time, and you know what happened? After a physical opening shift in which we dominated, "puny" Hamilton made tons of mistakes, couldn't find the answer to Colgate's systems, and lost 6–1.

There is more than one lesson to be learned from this personal story. First, bulletin-board material does not work. Actually, it is impossible for it to work. It provides the illusion of "firing up" a team when the genuine fuel for performance is inner clarity and calm, or stillpower. As we are aware, an external factor or judgment has no ability to impact a player's performance positively (or negatively), and the minute we look in that direction is the minute our ability to compete with precision starts to drift away.

The second lesson has even deeper practical applications. Today, in one locker room after another, coaches and athletes are making the mistake of looking outside of themselves in order to prepare for competition. Tactics such as making comments to the media or trying to inspire hatred of opponents are only serving to rev up thought and emotion—the exact opposite of the clear level of functioning necessary for long-term success and growth. As opposed to what many of us think is true, respect for (and cooperation with) opponents is what allows us to prepare and execute fully. Looking down on the opposition, or judging, will always have the opposite effect.

The crux of these two lessons, however, can be summed up in the following question: Isn't it simply time for players, coaches, and leaders in the sports world to start to dispel these longstanding motivational misconceptions? Not only because it feels right to do so—judgment and contention will always bind; respect and cooperation will always free—but because these motivational mistruths do not work. They have absolutely no power to contribute to the development of players or the enduring success of teams.

Judgment and What We Can Learn from the State of Mind of Two Great Players

By four PM on September 14, 2009, I had received eleven calls and twenty-four emails about the behavior of two famous athletes in regard to two separate events: Serena Williams lambasting an official for making a foot-fault call during the closing minutes of her US Open semifinal loss and Michael Jordan taking some parting shots at several old foes during his Basketball Hall of Fame induction speech. I had also read and listened to the comments of many sportscasters and columnists who were extremely critical of the "appalling" behavior of these two popular stars.

Many people that day wanted my opinion on the behavior of Williams and Jordan. And, as you can probably guess, I refused to answer the question. I believe that too many of us today—including Williams and Jordan, in these cases—are caught up in the habit of judging external situations and other people. As a result, we are creating unnecessary obstacles for ourselves. We are much better off following the examples of clear thinkers such as De Vicenzo, Robinson, and Burke.

Simply stated, nothing useful ever occurs when we judge the behavior of others. In fact, when someone is judged or condemned, that person often becomes angry and resistant, usually reinforcing the negative cycle of behavior. Why? Because, as I have mentioned, unproductive or deviant actions will always be the result of an individual's low psychological perspective in the moment—not the world around the individual. So when the same individual is judged or disciplined, since he is in a low place and not seeing or thinking clearly, it is impossible for him to grasp the purpose and lesson behind the judgment or discipline.

Once you understand that, you will also grasp another important reason to take stock in your own level of well-being moment to moment: Every situation you face is an opportunity either to react and apply judgment, or look deeper into what's really going on and offer compassion and a possible solution. Especially interesting is that the choice between these two courses of action has nothing to do with the person or encounter in question—it's all up to you.

I've often heard one of my mentors, George Pransky, facetiously, yet insightfully, say, "When I was younger and I met people who rubbed me the wrong way, I used to think there was something wrong with them." Applied here, how we see Williams, Jordan, or any individual has little to do with them; it's all about our own present state of mind. So while you may initially condemn the actions of these two "privileged" players, what do you think of them when your mind is still and peaceful? Even though you probably won't condone their actions, I believe you'll look at them with concern and perhaps kindness as well. When life is viewed from a perspective of clarity, it's impossible to feel the need to judge.

What then would my message be for Serena Williams and Michael Jordan in these situations? When under apparent duress, don't forget what got you to the top of your sport in the first place: a free and naturally persistent state of mind. From this psychological perspective, cooperation becomes paramount, judgment ceases, and external sources—opponents, a line call, or even retirement—will never be viewed as a threat.

The Negative Effect of Judging

I have to admit, I don't always practice what I preach. I often judge the habit of judging. That's because I understand the potential damage that looking down on someone else can inflict on a relationship, organization, or team. As discussed, individuals usually become defensive when judged, which empowers unproductive behavior. I have also said that those who judge fail to recognize their own low state of mind in the moment, since a person will never look down on others when his or her level of psychological functioning is elevated. However, here I want to demonstrate the far-reaching effect that judging, or refusing to judge, a team member or colleague can have on your team, organization, or yourself.

Years ago, when Brett Favre was a rookie quarterback for the Atlanta Falcons, head coach Jerry Glanville judged Favre to be irresponsible on and off the field. In fact, Glanville looked down on his "raw" quarterback from Southern Mississippi right from the start. When his feelings about not drafting Favre were overruled, Glanville even said it would take a "plane crash" for him to put Favre in a game. Then, when Favre missed the team photo that year, Glanville dubbed him a "train wreck," and following the 1991 season, the Falcons traded Favre to Green Bay.[5] And the rest, as they say, is history.

To the contrary, way back in the summer of 1970 at the University of Michigan, a freshman named Donnie Warner knocked on the door of head football coach Bo Schembechler's office. Standing five-foot-nine and weighing only 170 pounds, Warner asked for a meeting with the not-yet-legendary second-year coach. Warner wanted to try out for the football team.

Schembechler had a busy schedule but reasoned that any young man who had the guts to make a personal request like that deserved at least a few minutes of his time. Schembechler listened to "little" Donnie Warner state that he wanted to play offensive guard for one of the biggest and best college programs in the country. When Schembechler told him how huge the Michigan offensive line was, Warner's response was, "Okay, then I'll play defensive line—middle guard." Schembechler almost fell out of his chair.

Flash forward to Warner's senior year. By then, he had earned a full scholarship, was starting at middle guard, and was one of the leaders of the team. Until the day he died, Schembechler considered Donnie Warner the greatest Michigan player he had ever coached.[6]

So here are my requisite questions for coaches or leaders of any organization: Do you judge your players? What do you base your judgments on? What state of mind are you in when you judge a player or his performance? Are you too preoccupied with your own restrictive thoughts to notice that you might be in the company of an outstanding contributor (such as Favre or Warner)?

Glanville was so busy focusing on what was wrong with Favre, in spite of his obvious physical attributes, that he let Favre's potential wither away in Atlanta.

Whereas Schembechler was so busy appreciating what was right with Warner that he created an environment that helped Warner become one of the most revered players in Michigan football history—despite his having no tangible physical attributes. Schembechler was even quoted as saying, "Nothing demonstrates the value of giving a guy a chance [or not judging] more powerfully than the story of Donnie Warner."[7]

To me, it's plain to see: When we succumb to our errant thoughts or closed-off moods, judge another person, and then act from this egotistical perspective of insecurity, it is practically impossible to find long-term success. Glanville's record as a pro head coach was 63–73, while his subject of ridicule, Favre, has rewritten the NFL record book at the quarterback position. Schembechler's record at Michigan was 234–65–8, and while this total is pretty amazing in itself, the enduring relationships that he developed with his players are what he is truly remembered for.

The next time you find yourself in an apparent predicament and are tempted to look down on another, think about the real-life stories of Glanville and Favre, Schembechler and Warner. Realize that judging someone else says a lot more about you than it does about the person in question, and once you fall into the habit of negatively labeling others, it's difficult to turn back. If you are tempted to judge, the way out actually lies in looking *inward* toward your own thoughts and level of consciousness, not in reacting to the seemingly negative circumstances of the outside world. No matter the situation, if you can just hang in there and resist the ego's negative pull (and thus see life from the inside out), I can assure you that conviction and then hope will become a reality before you know it—just ask "raw" Brett Favre and "little" Donnie Warner.

8
MIND, BODY, AND PERFORMANCE

Well-being is not the fruit of something you do;
it is the essence of who you are.
MICHAEL NEILL

A college basketball coach once asked me to address his team about the state of mind of worry. The coach believed his players were underperforming due to their mental worry about upcoming tournaments and exams. As a result, they had just lost their third game in a row.

As many athletes and coaches can relate, it is always important to nip the worry factor in the bud. But, like most individuals seeking guidance today, this coach wanted me to help alter his team's mind-set by providing tips and training, which the players could apply when worry, and its physical manifestations, kicked in. Much to the coach's surprise, however, I told him I didn't have a pocket full of mind tricks to cure worry. I told him a person who worries does not have to train himself to do anything. If you actually try to do something to rid yourself of worrisome thoughts, you are repeating the common but self-defeating mistake of allowing yourself to be a victim of your own thinking. Remember, using a mental technique to train or change your own thoughts may work temporarily but, before long, it will only lead to more revved-up (or worrisome) thoughts, which will always lower your performance level.

The Only Way Out of Worry

The solution is to realize that worry, or anxiety, comes from your current judgments about a neutral external circumstance—it is not part of the circumstance. A championship game, for instance, can never be the cause of an athlete's anxious thoughts. These thoughts are only produced when his level of well-being is low. From this faulty psychological perspective, the athlete will never see life clearly, so he is more susceptible to his own misleading thoughts, incapable of solving apparent problems, and more prone to immersing himself in losing streaks or slumps.

Now, if you grasp this understanding, you have a profound resource at your disposal at all times. You see that any life situation combined with an insecure state of mind will always create the false impression of a problem—resulting in worry and/or stress. When you are in a low place, a comment made by an opposing basketball player or an official might appear worrisome or even ignite anger. Yet, the same comment made when your level of well-being is high might appear insignificant or even humorous. It is never the outside world (the championship game, the exam, your win-loss record) that regulates your level of happiness, your competitiveness, or your body's ability to perform. It's always your own thoughts and level of well-being in the moment.

Let's return to the quandary of what a coach, an athlete, or anyone is supposed to do when a low state of mind creates negative or worrisome thoughts. Once you recognize where your worries originate, you will also see that the worst thing you can do is look outside of yourself for a permanent solution. There is no pill that can truly calm your thoughts, no behavior modification that will help you, no affirmation (replacing a negative thought with a positive one) that can stop the worry.

In fact, I often suggest the following analogy, first introduced to me by friend and colleague Mara Gleason of One Thought, Inc.: When you are caught up in a progression of worry, understand that you are only walking through a haunted house, a place of illusion. Your life is not haunted. So the more you give in to the illusions (your worries), the longer your walk will take. In other words, although your worries look and feel real in the moment, they have nothing to do with the events of your life. Worries are deceptions of a low mind-set. Once you stop looking outside for a way to fix your worries, your level of well-being will ascend naturally. Then faith will take hold, anxious thoughts will fade away, and a return to the win column becomes possible.

The Connection—Explained

Understanding the role of thought and consciousness can provide deeper and more productive possibilities in many areas—from handling worry to explaining another hot topic in athletic circles today: the mind-body connection. A person's thoughts and mind-set, as this book has shown, have a tremendous impact on his or her physical ability to perform. In my own life, I sometimes find myself so wrapped up in an activity that I overlook an injury or sickness. And athletes who become deeply immersed in the experience of competition often fail to notice injuries until long after the game or practice has ended.

As a personal example of the connection between mind and body, my son Ryan, a collegiate baseball pitcher, recently underwent reconstructive elbow surgery (Tommy John surgery). When the doctor told us his injury had probably lingered for years, my wife and I were amazed. Pitching with an elbow that required such a major operation, Ryan performed at a high level and never once complained about pain.

How, you might ask, are athletes like Ryan able to perform like this? Well, a crucial and almost always misunderstood ingredient of the mind-body connection is that it never occurs consciously and can never be forced. An athlete (or anyone) can, in the moment, disregard a physical affliction by being immersed in an activity or a process (like pitching). However, it is virtually impossible to will the mind to do so. In John E. Sarno's popular book *The Mindbody Prescription*, he correctly illustrates that we can think our way into illness or injury, but I caution you against adopting the notion that we can think our way out of pain by controlling our thoughts.[1] No, the mind-body connection will not work in reverse.

As we have discussed, the principle of thought simply doesn't work that way. If you have an ailment and, like many well-intentioned athletes, try to rise above it by thinking positive thoughts, you will only rev up your mind, lower your consciousness, and in turn, greatly reduce the odds of conquering the pain. My son did not move through his elbow injury because he tried not to think about it or because he tried to think positively. He excelled on the mound because he lost himself in the process of pitching. In fact, if Ryan had focused on overcoming anything, there would have been little chance for him to throw even one pitch with his elbow in such a sensitive condition.

So, what is the proper way to use this mind-body connection? First, you must understand that there is no place in the mind-body connection for an athlete's ego. Too many players try to fight through pain or grind through discomfort when they should be listening to their own instincts. The issue of head injuries, in particular, has plagued athletes for years. And recently, the sports and medical communities have begun to educate today's players about the dangers. Yet, I believe most players, deep down, have always known that in succumbing to external pressures (their own ego or the ambitions of others) and quickly returning to the field following head trauma, they are playing with fire.

Still, to most athletes, various external pressures exist. As a result, they are sometimes confused about when to tough it out or when to shut it down. Not long ago, for instance, a football-playing client asked this straightforward question: "If I think I might be injured, how do I know if I should play or not?"

The answer, I told him, is much closer than you realize. Simply look inward to your state of mind in the moment. Regardless of the aches and pains, do you feel calm, are your thoughts lucid? Only from this mind-set will the player see an injury for what it truly is—either something that needs to be addressed or simply an overreaction.

Believe it or not, while pain certainly doesn't feel good, we know it has a purpose. It's an instinctive messenger telling us something is off course. It may be alerting us that we are bodily injured and need attention, or it may be a manifestation of an emotional challenge telling us to slow down. Far too many athletes, however, are still taking the field when their intuition is telling them otherwise. These are the players who will under-perform now and possibly set themselves up for a permanent injury that will last a lifetime.

Why Pain Will Never Lead to Gain

An athlete's innate ability to recognize true pain and injury is imperative in a sporting culture (and society) that promotes "motivational" philosophies such as no pain, no gain. One of my clients, who adhered to this philosophy, once wondered how she could help her young son turn the pain of tackle football practice into a positive experience. She insisted, "Football is not an easy sport; it takes hard work and comes with some pain." Her son, however, was having a difficult time believing football was supposed to be fun and productive, when at that moment his body was telling him otherwise.

From my perspective, the concept of no pain, no gain is old-school rhetoric that actually imperils athletes. If an athlete accepts this misguided attitude, he runs the risk of confusing his inborn understanding of how it is we improve, or get stronger, with the sensation of true pain, which is perfectly designed to tell him to back off or look elsewhere for fulfillment. Besides, as mentioned in chapter 2, if an activity is difficult and you have to force yourself to participate, then maybe you shouldn't be involved in the activity in the first place.

The most significant flaw in the no pain, no gain philosophy, though, is that it teaches athletes (or anyone) to try way harder than is necessary. Coaches and parents who adopt this view put the health of athletes at risk, hinder their ability to learn through the sports they play, and make it difficult for them to discover and pursue their passions freely. In other words, no pain, no gain is all about willpower and grinding it out. As I have said, a passionate person will never need willpower to fuel performance.

I instilled this message to the mother of the young football player by telling her that personal development and pain do not mix. I explained that all individuals grow from positive feelings; negativity is only a sign that we are about to head off course. Thankfully, she agreed. She decided it wasn't necessary to tell her son anything about the pain or hard work required to be a proficient football player; he would pursue what interested him and eventually find his own path to achievement.

What we should all learn from this illustration is much more general in nature: Yes, it is possible for an individual to excel at any endeavor to which he is introduced, but enduring success will only occur if the individual listens to his personal built-in navigation system—his own inner wisdom and instincts.

The Overlooked Secret to Avoiding Injury

Throughout sports history, many athletes have unknowingly possessed a deep understanding of the principles of the mind-body connection and have subsequently found remarkable success. Hockey great Wayne Gretzky, for example, weighed about 170 pounds during the better part of his career. He obviously played a bruising sport, was often the focus of the opposition's tough guy, and during the course of the season, logged an incredible amount of ice time. How then would you explain the fact that he was rarely injured during the twenty-two years he played professional hockey?

Roger Federer, one of the greatest tennis players of all time, still plays a grueling schedule in which his body is put to the test, tournament after tournament. Yet he continues to reach the finals or semifinals of most tournaments while playing against hungry younger rivals. What then is his key to staying healthy?

The answer lies in an overlooked and more profound aspect of the mind-body connection: Players with the keenest of mental games naturally conserve energy during play. When you are conserving energy, your body is far less susceptible to injury compared to those players who are constantly fatigued.

Since this notion might seem obvious, let's take a closer look at why athletes who play their sports with a relatively free-flowing state of mind rarely spend time on the disabled list. Players get hurt when their minds are not present or absorbed in the task at hand. Much like when we fail to live in the present in our daily lives, when an athlete dwells on a past mistake or worries about the future, he or she will get careless. When we get careless, we open ourselves up to being in the wrong place at the wrong time, and in the wrong physical position. You can figure out what often comes next. Clearly, the gift of living in the present moment has allowed both Gretzky and Federer to excel, but it also has enabled them to play their chosen sports longer.

There is one other factor that has significant implications in an athlete's quest to remain off the disabled list. And it is often confused by coaches, parents, and performers alike. Players who believe that they must force themselves into revved-up states of mind before games will be extremely vulnerable to injury. Athletes with tranquil minds, on the other hand, will compete with natural resilience and effort and tend to stay healthy regardless of age. In fact, look closely and you'll see that sports history is loaded with anecdotal evidence of the connection between longevity, success, and ease of mind. Think Cal Ripken, Martin Brodeur, Jerry Rice, Nancy Lopez, and Shaquille O'Neal.

A modern example of a pro athlete who exhibits this type of mind-set is another fine hockey player and the author of the foreword to this book, Zach Parise of the New Jersey Devils and the US Olympic team. I have had the good fortune to work with Zach over the past two years, and the power of a clear mind is one of our primary focuses. Now, if you have ever watched Zach play hockey, you know he never stops hustling, no matter the game situation. And even though he is more than willing to throw his body around, Zach is rarely injured. Up until the 2010–2011 season, he had only missed three games in his NHL career.

How then is it possible for a hockey player to put forth so much physical effort, night in and night out, and remain healthy? Zach's rigorous off-ice training program is part of the explanation, but more significantly, he is learning to play the game freely. When an athlete is in the zone or free, he actually hustles and conserves energy at the same time. That's productive hustle. Zach often finds himself in a positive position to make a pass or score a goal, and he's also less likely to be open for a hit (or to be in a compromising physical position when he is hit) that might lead to injury.

Plus, even if Zach happens to lose that feeling, he now understands that it's temporary; he allows his mind to calm (lets the glass sit). And with this self-correction in place, effort is easy once more.

• • •

If you are an athlete at any level, it is essential to train your body to avoid injuries. Understanding your mind for this overlooked purpose, however, is at least of equal relevance. A bound-up or tight level of *psychological* functioning leads to a bound-up or tight level of *physical* functioning, which will always lead to the susceptibility for injury. Just think about your own life experiences. When people are uptight, worried, or down, they tend to lack energy and often fall victim to illness. So, if you want longevity on the field of play, I suggest you develop an understanding not only of your physical attributes but also of the principles— revealed in *Stillpower*—that allow for an unencumbered, free-flowing, and keen state of mind.

9

EVERY ATHLETE'S BIRTHRIGHT

Failure is an interpretation, not a fact.
ALAN COHEN

A young hockey player and his father sat in my office one morning, full of questions and confusion. A senior in high school and an excellent player, this young man was struggling mightily with the decision to go to prep school the following year as a postgraduate or to play in the USHL, the leading junior hockey league in the United States. These days, in the world of college hockey, virtually all coaches require their recruits to take an extra year (or two) between high school and starting their college careers. So, while his college plans were all set for a year from now, he and his family were baffled about what to do in the coming season. They believed I could help shed some light on the predicament.

The Only Way to Decide

After we chatted for a while, the young man came right out and said, "Coach, if you were me, what would you do?"

I quickly responded, "Well, since I'm not you, I have no ability to answer that question, but let's talk about how I can help you uncover the answer for yourself." I then did something unusual. I took a quarter from my pocket and said, "I'm going to flip this quarter, and if it comes up heads, you're going to prep school. If it comes up tails, off to juniors you go." The father and son exchanged shocked glances. My reasoning was since the family had gone back and forth on the pros and cons of the choice numerous times, the only way to solve the apparent dilemma was to leave it up to chance. I then flipped the coin high into the air and, much to my delight, before it landed back in my palm, the young man blurted out, "I hope it comes up heads!"

I came away from this brief meeting with two lessons. First, if you are a coach, teacher, or parent, it is never helpful to make a direct decision for another person. The best mentors serve to bring out the inner wisdom in those they teach. The method that you use is solely up to you. Just keep in mind, part of your role is to help produce quality leaders, not quality followers.

Second, whenever you choose to intellectualize the positives and negatives of a decision, the answer always remains murky. Or, to be more exact: Pro-and-con lists take you farther away from a true answer, not closer. I suppose it's fine to think things through up to a point, but sooner or later your level of clarity, gut feelings, and inner knowledge must be consulted. Remember, you will never wrestle with a choice when your level of consciousness is high.

The bottom line on decision making is this: When we allow our thoughts to quiet, the answers, both on and off the field, will simply become obvious to us. Most of us believe that individuals who navigate smoothly through life do so by intellect. The truth, however, is that many intellectuals struggle mightily in their personal lives. To the contrary, our most effective ideas and actions occur via the calm mind-set of stillpower—when we're not trying hard to figure things out.

What I also realized that morning is that both coaches and players have profound requirements to live up to at decision time. A coach's job is to subtly bring forth a player's own ever-expanding inner knowledge. A player is obliged to see that productive decisions, including when to seek guidance, will only appear through the instinctive power of his or her own insight.

Switch-Hitting

The significance of this power occurred to me through an experience I recently had with my sixteen-year-old son, Jackson. Several months ago, a surprising insight about Jackson's baseball career popped into my head: I envisioned him as a switch-hitter. Jackson has fooled around in our backyard batting cage with this concept before, and he always plays Wiffleball Home Run Derby as a lefty with success, so why not give it a shot? He is a starting high school shortstop who dreams of playing college baseball, and surely college coaches are attracted to players who can hit from both sides of the plate.

However, when I excitedly mentioned this idea to my son, he thought I had totally lost my mind. While at first glance it seemed like the concept was intriguing to him, in the next instant, Jackson reacted and began spouting all the reasons why this change wouldn't work. He was too old to do it, he's a natural righty, and if he switch-hit, then he would be forced to bat lefty 85 percent of the time (because, as he estimated, 85 percent of high school pitchers are right-handed). Furthermore, his high school coach would never allow it. And finally, he added, "Dad, you must think that I'm not a good hitter for you to come up with this suggestion now!"

To put it simply, I was watching Jackson have a major thought meltdown right on the spot. One negative thought led to another, then another, and soon the idea that I had believed would help had been transformed into a threat against his baseball life.

Fortunately, I know better than to try to reason with anyone when his or her state of mind is all over the place. Jackson was definitely in no mood to hear that his thinking was distorted, and telling him that I was just making a loving suggestion would only rev up his state of mind even worse. So, I decided to step away from the situation and give my son some space, which was easy because Jackson didn't even want to look at me at that moment, much less talk.

The next morning the sun came up, my family had breakfast together, and we all went about our day. Several days came and went with not one mention of the switch-hitting suggestion. Then about a week later, I was sitting in my office working on this very book, when the following text message from Jackson came across my BlackBerry: "Shane Victorino [the Philadelphia Phillies' center fielder] started switch-hitting four years into his professional career." That's all he said. And that's all he needed to.

. . .

Many times when our thoughts, emotions, performances, or even our relationships go astray, we sense the need to come up with a solution, right on the spot. After all, if we don't feel right, why wouldn't we want to fix the feeling? In this book, however, we have seen that often the best answer is to do nothing in that moment, for what we really need is a little room to allow our psychological functioning to clear. Only then will we find the meaning and proper path to any apparent predicament.

What Jackson truly required was a little time to discover, independently, that finding a way to do something is always better than finding a reason not to—an incredible insight indeed. And by the way, he is really smacking it from the left side of the plate these days.

The Ridiculously Simple Way to Help Athletes Uncover Insight

I fully understand that, in the heat of the moment, giving athletes the necessary time and space to find their own insights, and thus answers, might seem impossible or unlikely to some parents, coaches, or even athletes. For example, I once gave a talk to a group of high school baseball players and their parents at a Baseball Factory event in Florida, and this subject became quite controversial.

During the open discussion portion of the evening, a father of one of the players asked me: "With all the rushing around we do these days, how can I offer more conscientious and focused advice to my kids?"

My answer, however, was not appreciated by this concerned gentleman. I simply said, "Just stop rushing."

In this want-it-and-need-it-now world, many of us have fallen into the trap of thinking there are certain things we *must* do and certain places we *must* get to. Subsequently, we are stifling our own instinctive ability to find reason. If you truly want to become a better coach, player, parent, or leader of any kind, then understand that no matter what you are thinking at any moment, there is nothing "out there" that you actually have to do. And if this suggestion has you scratching your head, just think about how successful you actually are not, when you do something that you don't want to do right from the start.

Let's take the all-too-familiar scenario of a typical father (and I've been there, too), who puts in eight hours at work and then rushes home to pick up his teenage daughter. The young girl has been in school all day, is now cramming for an exam, and has to be at a private softball lesson at seven PM at a facility four towns over. The father is fighting traffic, still consumed with work, and all he really wants to do is go home and have a relaxing dinner with his family. The daughter is also feeling overwhelmed with her responsibilities and can't figure out how she is going to get everything done: eat dinner, actually perform well in her lesson, study, and get a decent night's rest for the exam tomorrow.

It's been drilled into both father and daughter, though, that it's all about commitment. The harder you work at softball (no matter what), the more successful you'll become. So, against both of their better judgments they gulp down a few bites of dinner and dash off to the lesson. Because both father and daughter are now functioning with no clarity whatsoever, they get into a disagreement on the way: The father questions his daughter's respect, the daughter doesn't like being judged, they almost get into an accident, and they show up ten minutes late for a thirty-minute, and soon-to-be-fruitless, lesson.

What, exactly, would have been wrong with both father and daughter following their gut instinct and just staying home that night? In the madness of the moment, they both lacked the understanding that any decision you make is ultimately yours and yours alone. Despite what the world, your calendar, and your hazy thinking in the moment might say, we are all born with the free will to go down any path we choose at any time. In fact, I believe it is this understanding that allows us to be persistent and committed in the first place.

Let's now go back to the concerned parent who was put off by my succinct answer during my speech to the young baseball players. He sent me an email a short time later and said he had thought about my reply and realized the words were actually rather insightful. He mentioned his family was so busy trying to keep up that they often lost sight of why they did what they did in the first place. I thanked him for the note and then reminded him (and myself) always to be on the lookout for signs that we are acquiescing to the craziness of this go-go-go, always-on, one-click culture. When we adhere to the notion that there is something "out there" to chase, we lose perspective, make choices against our better judgment, and ultimately get careless.

The Issue with Visualization and Game Film

As you know by now, I am not a fan of performance tools, external self-improvement methods, theoretical processes, or prescribed routines that are supposed to promote serenity and positive thinking—when all they actually do is hamper a player's free will and creativity.

The answer to an athlete's optimal performance lies within him or her, not in the mirage of quick fixes. To illustrate, when great athletes speak of visualization or imagery, they are actually describing insights that simply come to them about an upcoming or past contest. These images appear naturally and are never forced, since seeing the path to great play will emerge when our minds are still and we allow it to happen. In describing this occurrence, Jack Nicklaus once said, "I never hit a shot, even in practice, without having a very sharp, in-focus picture of it in my head. It's like a color movie."[1] Yes, Nicklaus obviously did create in his own mind what he wanted to do prior to each shot. Yet the visualization was never forced. "I just do it. It happens naturally," he insisted.

The practice of visualization also often initiates the following predicament: There are many pro or collegiate athletes who have manifested exactly what they have visualized (like making it to the NFL) and still end up discontented or in trouble. I learned the following concept from Alan Cohen, and I am applying it here to the athletic arena. If you feel the need to use visualization as

a performance aid, then imagine how you want to feel—
not (as many coaches would recommend) the outcome
of a play, shot, or game. In other words, visualize the
feelings of poise, confidence, competitiveness, or teamwork; then the building blocks to those qualities will
reveal themselves in the proper way and at the appro -
priate time.

Perhaps a discussion about another commonly misunderstood and misused tool in sports today, dissecting
game film, will help to further demonstrate the tendency
of athletes and coaches to cramp their own creative
powers. If you are an athlete or coach who diligently
examines game video to try to correct or discover mistakes, you are most likely making your difficulties worse.
This statement may seem bold or brash, but in my experience, it is always true.

Several years ago a premier golf instructor on the PGA
Tour had an intellectually ingenious idea. After a player
won a tournament, he would fly to meet that player and
then film his golf swing. He reasoned that since the player
had just won, his swing had to be close to perfect. After all,
it is very difficult to win on the PGA Tour. Then, when the
particular player was struggling later with his game, he
could simply look at the old tape and compare the "right"
swing with the "wrong" swing and work to recapture

what he was doing well at the time of the victory. Seems like a great idea, right? But guess what. Most of the time the swings looked exactly the same, and sometimes the player was even swinging technically better when he didn't win. The only thing this program created was confusion and, with it, anxious thoughts for the player.

Likewise, I once worked with a college basketball player who was having trouble finding his scoring touch. As a result, he was toiling over videotape in a quest to discover what he was doing differently compared to the previous season, when he had averaged twenty-five points per game. But similar to the golfer's discovery, as he studied the tape, this player realized his positioning and technique were virtually identical, if not better, than the year before. And in the week after the video analysis, his scoring average had actually declined—a lot. "What the heck is going on?" he asked me.

What's going on is that sports teams and players today are using video for the wrong purpose. If you want to take advantage of all the advances in video technology, I encourage you to watch film, but please don't study it. When you study your performance on film, you are grinding. You are trying to compel change from an insecure state of mind instead of letting change come naturally (growth).

Here's the way to productively use sports film: When you watch video, you should be looking for an insight or a feeling, not a factual accounting of what is right or wrong with you or your team's play. For example, I recently advised a slumping hockey player to watch videos of the greatest scorers in NHL history instead of poring over his own game film. "Get a feel for what they are doing out on the ice," I told him. That exercise would pay off far more than his hurtful and intense self-examination in the heat of a scoring drought.

What might surprise you, in fact, is that some of the most successful Broadway performers actually refuse to watch videos of past shows, even though they are repeating the same lines and movements night after night. They understand each night is a new start with a different audience and ambiance. To keep the presentation fresh, the actors seek answers not in the past but in the present moment of each night's performance.

So, just like a stage performer looking to stay on top of his or her craft, recall that the past is merely a thought or memory carried through time. Trying to recreate it will take you right out of the present moment—and there goes your feel for the game. From this perspective, you are actually forcing yourself to use your intellect to perform. You are overthinking it.

When you watch game film, prepare for an upcoming contest, or aim to make any productive decision, what you are looking for is a quiet, clear, and elevated level of consciousness bound to produce that aha moment. When you rehash your performances or overthink the past or future, your thoughts tend to run wild, your consciousness plummets, and your troubles only get worse. It is, therefore, necessary to choose wisely the time, place, and state of mind for any type of self-reflection. And never forget, you are looking for an insight into making miracles happen *now*, in the present—not an intellectual accounting of an illusory past failure or future success.

10
THE FREEDOM TO WIN

Every individual possesses the potential to live and perform freely—no matter the circumstances of his or her life.
GARRET KRAMER

In the preceding pages, I have written about the clear state of mind that is necessary for teams, players, and coaches to become more competitive, consistent, and confident. And while my distinct mission is to help athletes find productivity and enjoyment through sport, I must mention, finally, that to me winning is extremely important, and it is clearly appropriate for an athlete or coach to possess the burning desire to beat his or her opponent.

At many levels of athletics, however, this message about winning is often blurred and confused. Take today's "everyone gets a trophy" mentality in youth sports—it distorts the true lessons and opportunities to mature that competition provides. There is a big difference, in my opinion, between it being okay to lose (not very often) and you being okay (always) if you happen to lose.

Said another way, only when an athlete deeply understands that an outcome has no ability to define him or her as an individual, will he or she have truly found the freedom necessary for long-term development and success. In stressing concepts such as "It's all about having fun," "Just do your best—winning is not important," or "We're all winners," youth sports leagues and parents are actually attempting to control the innocent participant's thought process. They are not allowing young athletes to draw their own insightful conclusions. If your daughter, for instance, believes that winning means something, then who are you to tell her that it doesn't?

Effort and the aspiration to excel are natural instincts. They cannot be dictated. So, I suggest we stay out of young players' ways. Let's provide the freedom for our kids to get on the field, stage, or any type of creative outlet; use their imagination; hustle; and go for it. I am certain that in an environment of clarity and free will, the fundamental lessons and attributes of sportsmanship, respect, and compassion for teammates (and opponents) will be uncovered at the appropriate place and time for each individual.

Eunice Kennedy Shriver, the founder of the Special Olympics, always insisted that every Special Olympic athlete take his or her participation in the games seriously. In her eyes, the inclusive nature of the events was not designed to relinquish the joy, diligence, and tears of true competition. Far removed from current youth leaders and parents, Mrs. Shriver knew that the freedom to win or lose was exactly what these misunderstood and challenged athletes needed for their personal growth. According to her son, Bobby, "Everyone told my mother that mentally challenged kids would start to cry if they lost. To which my mother responded, 'So what? That's what everyone does.' Her thought was: You compete, you exult if you win, you get sad if you lose, and you go back and try again."[1] Here is simple wisdom, for all of us, about our inborn potential to compete freely.

The Discovery

Several months ago, I received a joyous call that demonstrates the power of competing freely. It came from a baseball pitcher who first met with me because, in spite of numerous calming exercises prescribed by his team's sports psychologist, he continued to struggle on the mound. In his words, a fear of getting hit with a ball, a "comebacker," while finishing his pitching motion had developed seemingly out of nowhere. Throwing strikes had become difficult, and the more he tried to settle his fearful thoughts, the more fear he felt and the worse he performed.

The reason for the call was that during his last game, something changed. Even though he still had fearful thoughts, for some unexplainable yet empowering reason (remember the clout of insight), when the umpire yelled, "Play ball," he simply reared back and threw a "heater" right down the middle for a called strike. Eleven pitches later and with the fear of the comebacker waning, the pitcher realized he'd retired the opposing team 1-2-3. In my client's words, that night he made the amazing discovery that it was possible for him to perform to the best of his ability in spite of his fearful thoughts. Plus, the more he recognized his potential to do so, the freer he felt and the more competitive he became.

Indeed, over the course of the previous six months, this player and I had had numerous discussions about the principle of thought. He discovered that negative or fearful thinking, on its own, is entirely neutral and will only persist if a person fails to recognize his or her low level of consciousness at that moment. I helped him to see that his thoughts and feelings, whatever they may be, had no ability to encumber his life or performance in any way.

To get a sense of what I am talking about, think again about an external circumstance in your own life (like the comebacker) that you believe possesses the power to bring you down or hurt your chance for success. Maybe it's your coach's rules, your boss's demands, your parents' expectations, or the illness of a loved one. Then ask yourself: *Does this circumstance always thwart my ability to perform? Does the circumstance always produce insecure thoughts and feelings inside of me?*

The answers to these questions will help you understand that it's never the outside world—the comebacker, the rules, or the illness—that restricts your opportunity for success. Only your own fluctuating thoughts, born from your current level of psychological functioning, can make it look this way. In other words, state of mind is the source of experience—not the effect.

That's why the fear of the comebacker didn't always cripple my client. When his mood was high, fearful thoughts came and went; when his mood was low, fearful thoughts stuck. So, no matter what pop psychologists might say, it will always be ineffective to seek coping mechanisms for paper tigers that each of us construct, regardless of the circumstances of our past, present, or future. Once you discover that wayward thoughts have nothing to do with the situation at hand, you will realize that if you try to alter or calm these thoughts, the more real they will seem and the more your performance, and life, will suffer.

One of the main reasons I wrote *Stillpower* is for you to see that the potential to make this precise discovery rests within you, *right now.* No matter the circumstance, when fearful thoughts appear, remember: They are self-created and powerless on their own. Negativity (fear included) is just a sign to slow down; whatever you are thinking and feeling at that moment, whatever you see— it's not true. Keep your foot off the gas pedal and your state of mind will ascend on its own. Then, answers will become obvious—you will realize there is nothing "out there" to fear.

The Rock Game

A final and personally touching example of this fearless competitive wisdom takes me back to my own youth, when my brother and I vigorously competed in many sports. Eventually, I settled into my true passion (at the time) of playing hockey, which later became amateur golf. Through all the contests, training, and practice, though, perhaps the game I went after with the highest degree of daring abandon was an ingenious backyard baseball game created by my father. This game became a family tradition and was later dubbed the Rock Game by his grandchildren.

The Rock Game goes like this, and I would love for you to try it. Two or more players take turns fielding a play: a ground ball, a high fly, or a hard line drive. Each play is scored on a scale of 1–5. However, if you make a super-duper, once-a-season type effort, there is a chance for a 6. The game is played to one hundred, and my father served as the only judge for my brother and me. Later, I was the judge for my own children.

Complaining about a call or any negative language results in a five-point deduction, and it is the norm to tap gloves with your opponent as you sprint on and off the field. A great catch and throw are important, but persistence (hustle) and creativity (innovative plays) are weighed much more heavily. Oh, lest I forget, the game is called the Rock Game because in our backyard there is a large flat rock where the players stand as they await their turn.

Assuming you have the picture, you can only imagine what my brother and I went through whenever our father had time to oversee the battle. I am talking about blood, sweat, and many bumps and bruises. We competed so freely and easily that, in the moment, nothing in the world mattered but catching, throwing, and hustling our rear ends off. Now, flash forward thirty years: I am happy to say that when my sons were slightly younger (they are eighteen and sixteen now), they took this competition to a whole new level. Baseball is their sport and current passion, and I am certain the Rock Game is one of the reasons why.

Of course, the Rock Game helps with the basics of catching and throwing a baseball. But more important, my father was perceptive enough to realize that in stressing effort, creativity, and poise, we were allowed to learn significant life lessons in our own way. My brother and I uncovered in ourselves the art of being persistent, while at the same time knowing it was potentially positive to make a mistake. And in understanding the relevance of keeping our composure (or risk a five-point penalty), we became aware that permitting our thoughts to settle gave us the opportunity to overcome any seemingly negative situation. This game is so etched in my mind that I can vividly remember competing full bore, but with such a sense of freedom, peace, and simplicity, that I both cared and didn't care about winning—at the exact same time.

I suppose the reason I recall these brilliant memories, much like the reason I wrote this book, is not to dwell on them, but to illustrate how powerful reflection and insight can be. I now look at this innocent game, created by my father, and realize how conscious we were in play and the unlimited lessons that were at our disposal. Today, when I watch my own children compete— my sons, Ryan and Jackson, on the baseball field, and my daughter, Chelsea, as she plays field hockey and lacrosse—I look for signs that they are expressing their freedom fully, that they are trying their best and desire to win. But above all, I want them to perform with composure, allowing their imaginations to soar. The Rock Game represents truth in competition for my family and me—pure wisdom in action. Looking back, it set the stage for the formation of this book and for the principles that I now hold so dear.

The Principles

Mind, consciousness, and thought. Throughout this book I have used real-life examples from the world of sports to portray the vast potential of these principles. To me, they are the essence of stillpower. Understanding the spiritual power of the mind, the sincere possibilities of being aware, and the illusory quality of thought are what allowed my brother and me (and my children) to compete at our fullest capabilities during the Rock Game and at every other moment when we were at our best. These principles, I believe, are perfectly and naturally designed to do the same for you.

About forty years ago, Sydney Banks had that aha moment. He had a spectacular revelation about the human experience. This insight not only has the capacity to enhance performance in athletics or any endeavor, but once uncovered and understood, it allows all individuals to navigate smoothly through life and to appreciate the journey along the way.

Now, Syd's revelation is not a technique or theoretical model; he was not a guru. Quite the opposite. The principles of mind, consciousness, and thought rest deep within all of us and can never be taken away. Syd realized this enduring message, and perceptive thinkers like George Pransky later ran with it. For some fortunate reason, I found my way to George and his colleagues and have since committed my life's work to introducing the infinite promise of these principles to the athletic community at large. I feel privileged to present this book as a continuation of that process.

One last word of advice on the principles: Since *Stillpower* doesn't elaborate on the definitions of mind, consciousness, and thought, I urge you to pick up a copy of one of Sydney Banks's most poignant books, *The Missing Link*. As a matter of fact, a copy sits on both my writing desk and my nightstand at home. It's not a sports book, but I have successfully recommended this simple but profound writing many times over the years. Please relish and enjoy it over and over again.

Your Journey, Your Way—So Long for Now

I now come full circle from where this book started, back to what is truly wondrous about sports in the first place: the journey. We all have the opportunity to take the field freely, compete wholeheartedly, and make the athletic and life experience entirely our own.

Yet, as the Rock Game insightfully showed me a long time ago, at times it will appear as if the competition, or even life, is not working out as planned. These are the moments when you must remember: External how-tos, hypothetical strategies, performance tools, or self-help techniques can never be successful supplements in your quest. Like all outside solutions, they represent coping mechanisms, shortcuts, or illusions that—in contrast to the Rock Game—overwork your natural thought system and sap your ability to figure things out for yourself.

To the contrary, the answers are always accessible; they can be found in the principles that rest deep within *you*.

Sadly, virtually all of us today, even our kids, believe we need to try our darnedest to find the secrets to success. We are laboring and revving, pushing and working, all at the expense of the most precious innate characteristic that every human being possesses: free will. Relying on willpower thwarts our instincts. It makes molehills into mountains, undermines our creativity, and weakens our ability to prevail.

There is an answer, however. The path to fulfillment will emerge, but only from the clarity and quiet of your unbounded imagination. Once again, reflect on your most awesome performances of any kind. Did you try hard to get there? Did you grind out the triumph? Or were you free? No matter your age or life history, that freedom, abundant determination, and resilience have really never left you. Empowering personal insights are waiting to pour out.

Sure, in writing this book, my hope is that your performance on the athletic field, at home, at work, or in school does improve. Although in a more profound way,

I want you to stop trying so hard to get there. See that the more open, responsive, and loving you are, the easier it will be to create your personal vision for achievement. Realize that your relationship with your own thoughts, and not the circumstances of life, will enhance your ability to move through any condition that confronts you. In the end, this understanding alone will determine your level of well-being and the quality of the contributions that you make to your team, community, or family.

Remember, the journey is only as difficult as you want to make it. Why use force when stillpower makes the game and life flow fluently? The time has finally come to stop toiling away at the strategies and methodologies of others. Simply look within to your own inner wisdom and understanding. Permit your own spirit and freedom to take you to new levels of performance, productivity, and contentment. *Excellence is so much closer than you think.*

EPILOGUE

THE ONLY ANSWER

Noticing when your thoughts are flowing—as opposed to getting stuck—will be the first sign that the central message of *Stillpower* is starting to take hold. It will be very subtle, especially at first, but ultimately it's only your own thoughts that possess the power to bring you down or raise you up. Not your coach, parents, teammates, amount of playing time, or even the past—only your own moods and resulting thoughts have that power.

When our minds race, we tend to take outside events at face value—forget they're neutral—and that's when we stumble. Always keep the following perspective in mind: Human beings intuitively understand how to move through their own errant thoughts, but they will always fail if fault is placed on external events or people.

As you are now aware, the trick is simply to take stock in yourself. *Are my thoughts clear? Are my feelings right? Am I open to life's big picture?* There is an extremely moving and true-to-life scene in the movie *Invictus* that vividly demonstrates this understanding.[1] In the movie, the year is 1995, and South Africa's president, Nelson Mandela—a man who deeply embodies the principles detailed in this book—orders the national rugby team to stage a series of youth rugby clinics all across his embattled country. At first, the team protests vehemently. The tour will take them away from their necessary training routine for the upcoming World Cup, which South Africa is hosting.

The players are certain, in the moment, that they must narrow their focus in order to find success. They are angry and disheartened; their collective level of consciousness is fading fast. However, the team captain, Francois Pienaar, knows better. In the midst of the storm, he looks within his own heart. He decides that the team will oblige the distinguished president. Just weeks before the competition, the players reluctantly embark on their tour.

The first stop is a shantytown of rundown buildings and athletic fields, and as the team bus arrives, the players become even more enraged. One player mutters under his breath, "We've broken training camp for this?" But slowly, as they make their way among the children, a transformation takes place. The eager youngsters swarm the sole nonwhite player on the team—a common bond is formed. The other players are touched; they realize what their presence truly means to these fellow South Africans. Their hearts, minds, and vision expand. They play with the children and teach them rudimentary rugby skills. Time seems to stop; the team's purpose becomes clear.

The entire nation grows to love its rugby players, and a sense of pride infuses the team. President Mandela's dream, his insight, takes shape—there's always reason to hope. Miraculously, the host team pulls off the upset; South Africa wins the World Cup. The joy is immeasurable—beyond the description of words.

. . .

I ask you now: Where was this magnificent success born? Did it come from focus, from selfishness, from the compulsion to train? No. It sprang from the highest level of human psychological functioning: the feelings of cooperation, resilience, and compassion. It came from love. It came from stillpower.

ACKNOWLEDGMENTS

About fifteen years ago, I journeyed from Newark, New Jersey, to La Conner, Washington. As I drove from the Seattle airport to the offices of Pransky & Associates, I called my dear friend Brian Day and said, "I don't know what's going to happen out here, but the way I feel at this moment, I'm open to anything." About an hour later, I met George Pransky. What I learned that day changed my life forever.

In addition to George, over the years there have been many coaches, teachers, authors, and friends who have helped shape my perspective and message. I am particularly grateful to the following: Alan Cohen, the late

Richard Carlson, and the late Sydney Banks, thank you for writing the words that initiated my quest. Keith Blevens was a wonderful teacher; he instilled the understanding, allowing me to find my own inner wisdom. Zach Parise and Rob Semerano showed tremendous faith and confidence in me; thank you both for being such quick learners. Nikki Nieves helped organize the chapters of this book and was a trusted partner throughout the process. Thank you, Nikki, for your insightful assistance. Sherry Roberts provided excellent editing advice and amazing patience. My appreciation for her contribution to this project is beyond description. Rodrigo Corral, thank you for stepping in and providing such perfect design elements and direction.

I also want to mention and thank the following extraordinary people: John Baiocco and the Capax Global team, your friendship, generosity, and hospitality will not be forgotten. Regina Mongelli, you've been the brains behind the operation for years—without your effort, none of this would be possible. Kristina Holmes, my agent and friend, your guidance and belief continue to be invaluable. Cynthia Black, Judith Curr, Richard Cohn, Lindsay Brown, Devon Smith, and Emily Han of Beyond Words/Atria Books/Simon & Schuster, thank you for embracing the concept of stillpower and for your faith in this project. Brian Day, the best hockey coach at any level today, you have set remarkable examples of resilience and courage. I am fortunate to have such a clear-thinking and cherished friend throughout the journey.

Now to my family. Claire Davis, thank you for showing me, a long time ago, that the answers would be found only if I looked inward. Fortunately, I found the freedom to notice. Paul Kramer is the person who, among many things, introduced me to all the joys that coaching can bring. We will always share this love. Sheila Mack, my mother-in-law and friend, your unwavering support and clarity mean the world to me. Rich LeFurgy's guidance was essential to the formation of Inner Sports. Thank you, Rich, for always being there. Karen LeFurgy and Robert Kramer, in spite of our challenging circumstances, you provided so many loving childhood memories. I continue to draw insights from them every day.

Finally, to Ellie, my beautiful wife, thank you for encouraging me to write *Stillpower* and sharing the adventure with me. And to my children—Ryan, Jackson, and Chelsea—I am the luckiest person alive to be your father. May you always hold the underlying message of this book dear to your hearts. It is born out of my love for you.

APPENDIX

YOUR GAME PLAN FOR THE FUTURE

In *Stillpower*, you have seen that the ultimate performance tools—your instincts, inner wisdom, and insights—rest within you. However, if you happen to get stuck and struggle in the moment, feel free to use the following inside-out reminders to help you get back in the game. They will point you away from external quick fixes and toward your own natural understanding.

1. *Only when you feel a sense of cooperation with your teammates, coaches, and even your opponents will you be mentally prepared to compete to the fullest extent possible.*

A person's life experience, or performance, is not the source of his state of mind; it is the effect. Looking at other people or events with disdain only serves to bind the mind and body of an athlete. When you are open to the productive possibilities in everyone and everything, your freedom—and effort—will soar.

2. *Struggles only occur when you are not operating from a clear mind-set. So when you attempt to solve problems from this state of mind, your performance will only get worse.*

We all fall into the trap of trying to fix a negative feeling or situation in the heat of the moment. But always to no avail. The purpose of negativity is to tell you when you're headed in the wrong direction. Stop stepping on the gas when your tires are stuck in mud. The human mind will self-correct to clarity and consciousness—if you allow it. Then the answers will easily appear.

3. *A coach's words are much less important than the state of mind from which the words are spoken.*

Here's a simple reminder: Words are merely an echo of a feeling. You might say to a player, "I was really proud of your effort tonight." But if there is no passion or love behind the words, they might actually have a negative impact. Coaches: Take note of your own level of functioning, moment to moment. Positive feelings and words originate only from positive states of mind.

4. A coaching methodology that focuses on behaviors is mentoring after the damage has already been done.

Poor performances or behaviors are the result of a player's low level of well-being. Nothing more, nothing less. Rather than holding players accountable for their actions, hold them (and yourself) accountable to recognizing the thoughts and feelings that accompany high levels of well-being—and only acting from this mental state. Then watch what happens to the performance level of your team.

5. Recognize the difference between your life situations and your life.

The quality of your life situations—your performances, your relationships, your finances—will always vary. Your life, however, is a constant. The best athletes understand that their life situations possess no ability to infiltrate their life. As bad as they want to win, if they don't, their life will be perfectly okay. This understanding will determine your ability to perform in the clutch.

6. *Keep goal setting in perspective.*

The more focused you are on the "prize," the more you thwart your awareness, shrink the perceptual field, and limit the imaginative possibilities. Achieving your goals will not elevate your level of self-worth or happiness. Relish the journey—the relationships and experiences. Then the path toward creating exactly what you want will become evident.

7. *Without the free will to choose, you will lack the resources to draw upon personal insights and move through errant emotions.*

Freedom is the number one ingredient to contentment and success, and it has nothing to do with your circumstances. The more you realize that external situations have no ability to regulate your independence, actions, and decisions, the more insights will flow and the more you will stay ahead of the competition.

8. The opportunity always exists to move through any situation successfully, no matter how challenging it might appear.

Everything that occurs in your life is meant to show you the way, not get in your way. When you are thinking clearly and your state of mind is high, life's purpose becomes obvious no matter what you face. Embrace the challenges by keeping this understanding in mind. The obstacles will make sense to you in no time.

9. Understand that no matter what you are thinking at any moment in time, there is nothing you actually have to do.

Effective actions are born from mental clarity, stillness, and a positive feeling. When these qualities are absent, an athlete will always feel the need to force it: to train incessantly, study game film, or look for some outside remedy to fuel success. If you go 0 for 5 in a baseball game, it's understandable to want to improve. Just remember, your time in the batting cage will only be productive if it's applied from the feeling of determination—not compulsion.

10. You will perform to the best of your ability from the ease, simplicity, and peacefulness of stillpower.

External performance techniques will always cloud the thinking and intuitive functioning of an athlete. The only source of the zone is your own inner wisdom. If you are not performing well, it is only because you continue to obstruct your own insights by relying on the psychological strategies of other people. Be still and look within—the answers are present, even if you can't see them at this exact moment.

Many thanks for reading these words. Good luck!

NOTES

Preface

1. Sydney Banks, *The Missing Link* (Auburn, WA: Lone Pine Publishing, 1998), 3.

Chapter 1

1. Betsy Stevenson, "Title IX and the Evolution of High School Sports" (research paper, The Wharton School, University of Pennsylvania, October 2007): http://bpp.wharton.upenn.edu/betseys/papers.asp.

2. Richard Carlson, *You Can Be Happy No Matter What* (Novato, CA: New World Library, 1992), 137.

3. Garret Kramer and Aaron Turner, "Why Current Thinking About the Mental Game Is Wrong, and What We Can Do About

It," GarretKramer.com, March 9, 2010, http://www.garretkramer .com/articles.

Chapter 2

1. Joe Pelletier, "'Mr. Goalie' Glenn Hall," Blackhawks Legends (blog), GreatestHockeyLegends.com, http://blackhawkslegends .blogspot.com/2006/09/mr-goalie-glenn-hall.html.

Chapter 3

1. Mike Krzyzewski, *Beyond Basketball: Coach K's Keywords for Success* (New York: Business Plus, 2006), 105–107.

2. Alan Cohen, *Wisdom of the Heart* (Carlsbad, CA: Hay House, 2002), 31.

3. Wayne Dyer quotes, 2012, http://www.brainyquote.com/quotes/ authors/w/wayne_dyer_2.html.

4. Tom Coughlin and Brian Curtis, *A Team to Believe In* (New York: Random House, 2008).

5. Sydney Banks, *The Missing Link* (Auburn, WA: Lone Pine Publishing, 1998), 93.

6. Angelo Pizzo, *Hoosiers* (Los Angeles: Orion Pictures, 1986).

7. Alan Cohen, *The Dragon Doesn't Live Here Anymore* (New York: Ballantine Books, 1993), 90.

Chapter 4

1. Alan Cohen, *Wisdom of the Heart* (Carlsbad, CA: Hay House, 2002), 116.

2. Steve Phillips, interview by Matt Lauer, *The Today Show* (New York: NBC, February 8, 2010).

3. Robert Rotella, *Golf Is Not a Game of Perfect* (New York: Simon & Schuster, 1995), 35.

4. Ibid., 36.

5. Sydney Banks, *The Missing Link* (Auburn, WA: Lone Pine Publishing, 1998), 47.

6. Michael Neill, *Supercoach* (Carlsbad, CA: Hay House, 2009), 45.

Chapter 5

1. Associated Press, "Hanley Ramirez Benched for Shockingly Lazy Play," TheHuffingtonPost.com (May 18, 2010): http://www.huffingtonpost.com/2010/05/18/hanley-ramirez-benched-fo_n_579859.html.

2. John Andrisani, *Think Like Tiger* (New York: Penguin Putnam Inc., 2002), 20.

Chapter 6

1. Daniel H. Pink, *Drive: The Surprising Truth About What Motivates Us* (New York: Riverhead Books, 2009), 44.

Chapter 7

1. Alan Cohen, *Wisdom of the Heart* (Carlsbad, CA: Hay House, 2002), 58.

2. Jackie Robinson quotes, http://famousquotesabout.com/quote/There_s-not-an-American/244568. Accessed February 2011.

3. Duke Snider quotes, http://www.baseball-almanac.com/quotes/quosnid.shtml. Accessed February 2011.

4. Jackie Robinson quotes, http://www.baseball-almanac.com/quotes/quojckr.shtml. Accessed February 2011.

5. David Mosse, "What if the Falcons Had Not Traded Brett Favre?" ESPN.com (February 20, 2007): http://sports.espn.go.com/nfl/news/story?id=2772472.

6. Bo Schembechler and John U. Bacon, *Bo's Lasting Lessons* (New York: Business Plus, 2007), 142–150.

7. Ibid., 142.

Chapter 8

1. John E. Sarno, *The Mindbody Prescription* (Warner Books, Inc., 1998).

Chapter 9

1. Jack Nicklaus, "Quote on Visualization by Jack Nicklaus," BeautifulSummerMorning.com (April 27, 2008): http://beautifulsummermorning.com/2008/04/quote-jack-nicklaus-visualization.

Chapter 10

1. Jack McCallum, "Eunice Kennedy Shriver 1921–2009: Altruist and Athlete, the Special Olympics Founder Saw the Uplifting Power of Sports," *Sports Illustrated*, vol. 111, issue 7, August 11, 2009.

Epilogue

1. Anthony Peckham, *Invictus* (Burbank, CA: Warner Bros. Pictures, 2009).

INDEX

CONTACT INFORMATION

Remaining accessible to those individuals in need, or to anyone with a comment or question, is very important to me. Therefore, please feel free to reach out. My email address is: gkramer@innersports.com.

To learn more about *Stillpower* or read articles written by Garret Kramer, please visit garretkramer.com.

I look forward to hearing from you, and I will respond.

ABOUT THE AUTHOR

Garret Kramer is the founder and managing partner of Inner Sports, LLC. His revolutionary approach to performance has transformed the way players, coaches, professional teams, and even parents view the athletic journey. Kramer lectures widely on the states of mind that lead to success on and off the playing field. He has been featured on ESPN, WFAN, FOX, and CTV as well as in national publications such as the *New York Times*, the *Wall Street Journal*, and *Sports Illustrated*. Kramer lives in northern New Jersey with his family.